JESUS

AND THE

COSMOS

Denis Edwards

Wipf & Stock
PUBLISHERS
Eugene, Oregon

Wipf and Stock Publishers
199 W 8th Ave, Suite 3
Eugene, OR 97401

Jesus and the Cosmos
By Edwards, Denis
Copyright©1991 Paulist Press
ISBN: 1-59244-763-5
Publication date 7/22/2004
Previously published by Paulist Press, 1991

Contents

Preface

This book involves the world of science as well as theology, and while I have found reading and reflecting on cosmology exciting, it has been an entrance into a whole range of disciplines which are not my own.

For this reason I am particularly grateful to Professor Alistair Blake, of the physics department of Adelaide University, who generously agreed to discuss with me the ideas contained in this book, and who provided me with critical suggestions and much encouragement. Robert Simons C.M., professor of systematic theology at St. Francis Xavier's Seminary, has also given me a valuable critical response to this work and much support. We have collaborated on work in this area on a number of occasions. There have been many other collaborators: people who have discussed these ideas with me in workshops and classes, Michael Trainor, who shares a home and many theological discussions with me, and other dear friends who have been my companions in this work. We have learned much from each other. I am very grateful to them.

Quotations from the Sacred Scriptures are from the Revised Standard Version (copyright 1946, 1952, 1971, 1973, by the Division of Christian Education of the National Council of Churches of Christ in the U.S.A.), except for two instances where I have made my own translation. Longer quotations from the works of Karl Rahner are taken from his *Theological Investigations,* published by Seabury Press, and are used by permission of the publishers.

I would like to thank Mrs. Joan Allen for her generosity and hospitality. This book is dedicated to Mark and Kath Edwards, who taught their children that the universe is filled with love.

1

Introduction

The Garden Planet

As the spacecraft Voyager 2 explored Neptune, a journalist expressed the hope that the knowledge gained on this journey would alert human beings to the vulnerability of Earth, "a tiny garden threatened by nuclear warfare, the greenhouse effect and destruction of the ozone shield."[1]

Viewed from lifeless planets like Neptune, and seen against the background of giant galaxies, the Earth is well described as a tiny, precious garden in space. This is a beautiful and an apt image for our planet. At the end of the twentieth century the Earth is like an abundant garden which is under threat on all sides.

The threat comes mainly from the human community who inhabit the garden. Men and women, when they first emerged from within the garden, tended to feel that the garden which encompassed them was endlessly bountiful. They assumed that it was inexhaustible. Gradually through ingenuity and intelligence they began to understand more and more of the processes of the garden and to manipulate them to their own advantage.

The human population grew. Human beings fought for dominance in the garden. Some groups gained control over more and more of what the garden produced, and claimed this was their due. Men dominated women, and claimed that this was right and natural. More powerful groups used more and more of the garden's resources, while others were reduced to misery.

Areas of the garden began to turn into desert. Life forms that had taken millions of years to evolve disappeared forever. The water system became polluted with waste. The atmosphere was damaged and the trees which had purified the atmosphere were being destroyed.

Numbers of women and men became conscious that the garden was under threat. They began to see that if things went on unchecked all life could be destroyed. The garden would become barren and empty. All living creatures would die. Human beings would be unable to survive.

There were different reactions to this new awareness. One reaction, particularly from those who were profiting most from controlling the resources of the garden, was to argue that the problem was being exaggerated. They used a number of arguments: human beings have the right to exploit the garden; the garden has probably got more resources than we know; human ingenuity would find a way to deal with the problem. Meanwhile they continued to exploit the garden.

Others reacted strongly. They saw through the false arguments of the first group, and understood that greed and selfishness were at the bottom of them. They were terrified at what human beings were doing to the garden. They believed that human beings had made a fundamental mistake in seeing themselves as at the center of things. They saw humanity as an arrogant and dangerous species. They distrusted human technology and human wisdom. They wanted to return to an older style of life, where humans were part of the whole life of the garden. Instead of dominance and arrogance there would be respect for the rhythms of nature.

There were others in the garden who were just as alarmed as the second group, but who believed that human beings had to use their ingenuity and their combined wisdom to find a way to care for the whole garden, and for each person in it. Like the second group they believed that humans were part of the garden, profoundly related to every other creature in it. But they understood human beings as the conscious, thinking dimension of the garden. They were very aware of damage done to the garden by human greed. They believed, nevertheless, that human beings had to take responsibility for the garden.

Those who held this third position were conscious of a great crisis in the garden. They were convinced that the abuse of the garden itself was connected to problems within the human community. They saw it as related particularly to two facts: first, that there was much hunger and suffering in the garden while small groups controlled and used far more than their share; second, that the women of the garden had long been dominated by the men. They were hopeful that human beings could respond to the crisis. They believed that this response would involve care for the garden, justice in the sharing of resources, and justice and mutuality between female and male.

The Theological Response

This book is an attempt at a response to the crisis facing the Earth at the end of the twentieth century from a theological perspective. It is an attempt to think theologically about this crisis in the light of the great Christian tradition.

It is important to remember that our theological tradition has been shaped within the worldview of a static universe. The great theological synthesis of St. Thomas Aquinas, for example, was formed within a culture which took for granted that the world was fixed and static, that the Sun and the Moon and the five known planet stars revolved around the Earth in seven celestial spheres, moved by angels, that beyond these seven spheres there were the three heavens, the firmament (the starry heaven), the crystalline heaven, and the empyrean, and that there was a place in the heavenly spheres for paradise. It was assumed that human beings were the center of the universe, that Europe was the center of the world, and that the Earth and its resources were immense and without any obvious limits.

By contrast, we are told today that the universe began with a cosmic explosion called the Big Bang, that we live in an expanding universe, with galaxies rushing away from us at an enormous rate, that the Earth is a relatively small planet revolving around the Sun, that it is hurtling through space as part of a Solar system which is situated toward the edge of the Milky Way galaxy, that we human beings are the product of an evolutionary movement on the Earth, and that we are intimately linked with the health of the delicately balanced life-systems on our planet.

The shift between these two mindsets is enormous.[2] It needs to be stressed that most of our tradition has been shaped by the first of these, and even contemporary theology has seldom dealt explicitly with the change to a new mindset. Teilhard de Chardin attempted to bridge this gap by forging a remarkable sythesis between science and theology.[3] Teilhard's vision, I believe, has still much to say to us in a new time. It is far from exhausted. But the very fact that the vision was erected on the basis of both science and theology means that it fails to satisfy completely either scientists or theologians.

Karl Rahner, who obviously had sympathy for the project of Teilhard's life, attempted to deal with many of the same issues from a strictly theological perspective. Rahner attempted to construct a Christology from within an evolutionary context. What comes as something of a surprise in rereading Rahner is the extent to which evolutionary and cosmic themes appear throughout all of his work. It is also interesting to note the extent to which Rahner seems to have been in touch with developments in modern physics.

Rahner's evolutionary anthropology and Christology have not received the attention they deserve. This was due, in part, to the urgent need to develop liberation and political theology in the 1960s and 1970s. As these theologies rightly took center stage, evolutionary concerns tended to fall from favor. There were even some who (unjustly, in my view) criticized the evolutionary work of Teilhard and Rahner as being naively optimistic, and not taking seriously enough the forces of oppression at work in our world.

In the 1990s we have no choice but to face up to the ecological crisis which confronts us. Religious thinkers like Thomas Berry are searching for a new synthesis of science and faith, a new cosmology, and a "new story."[4] Berry has much to contribute on these issues. In this book I would like to focus more directly than Berry on what the Christian tradition itself, and Christology, can offer us in the present crisis. Sean McDonagh writes as one who shares some of the perspectives of Thomas Berry, but also as a person who has been immersed in the pastoral and social world of the island of Mindanao in the Philippines. He has issued a strong and effective call to rethink Christian theology from the perspective of care for the Earth.[5]

Matthew Fox has been advocating a "creation spirituality" for our age.[6] He has drawn attention to the Christian mystical tradition, and its celebration of creation. He has been an effective publicist for the need for a more holistic and integrated approach to faith and life. Fox emphasizes creation over against redemption, and the cosmic Christ over against the historical Jesus. As will become clear in this book, I think it important to develop the intrinsic inter-relationship between creation and redemption, and between the historical Jesus and the Cosmic Christ.

Michael Himes and Kenneth Himes have joined forces to work toward an environmental theology. Their approach is to understand the whole of creation as a sacrament of the love of God. They advocate the idea of "companionship" between human beings and other creatures as a central component of a new ethics.[7]

European theologians, like Jurgen Moltmann from Germany and Gabriel Daly from Ireland, have been attempting to rethink the theology of creation from our new context.[8] Kathryn Tanner has discussed the specific issue of the inter-relationship between God's creative activity and the free actions of creatures, and the theological rules that apply to this issue.[9]

Feminist theologians, like Rosemary Radford Ruether and Sallie McFague, have had a major impact on our understanding of creation.[10] They inter-relate feminist concerns with ecology in a systematic way, and they consistently advocate a more holistic approach to larger theological issues.

Arthur Peacocke, a biochemist and an Anglican priest, has written creatively about the interconnection between modern biology and theology.[11] In quite a different way Charles Birch and John Cobb have brought together insights from both biology and holistic theology to develop an ecological understanding of life.[12]

John Polkinghorne, another Anglican priest, combines a professional interest in physics with Christian theology in a number of helpful books.[13] Daniel Liderbach has attempted to show a relationship between the discoveries of modern physics and the kingdom of God proclaimed by Jesus.[14]

In Latin America some theologians, like Juan Luis Segundo, have begun to develop the connections between the approach and themes of liberation theology and issues of cosmology.[15] Segundo interprets the limited options we find in the life of Jesus, and in Christian political practice today, in terms of the limits that emerge from an understanding of evolutionary history, and in terms of scientific concepts like entropy.

All of these developments have something to say to our current ecological crisis. It seems to me, however, that what Rahner has to contribute is often overlooked in the present discussion. Moreover I believe that some of the key insights that Rahner developed in the 1950s and 1960s have a new relevance and urgency in the situation of the 1990s. Christian believers of this generation have a crying need for theological insight into cosmology and evolutionary history.

Not only has modern science given this age a new cosmology, but contemporary historical studies have provided people of this same era with a new approach to the historical Jesus. Critical biblical study has allowed us to know far more than previous generations about the Jesus who brought joy and liberation into people's lives, at least forty years before the first gospel was written.

It is the purpose of this book to reflect upon the new story of the cosmos, in the light of the story of Jesus that emerges from historical studies, and to do this by way of some insights from the work of Karl Rahner. In this process I hope to take Rahner's insights a little further.

Outline of the Book

It is obvious that theology must listen to what science has to tell us about the story of the universe. The second chapter of this book, then, will be a brief summary of what we know from various twentieth century sciences, including astronomy, physics, geology and palaeontology. This overview will be limited by space and the competence of the writer. Nevertheless it is indispensable for the purpose of this book.

In the third chapter I will bring this scientific story of creation into dialogue with three principles from Rahner's theology. These principles concern the place of human beings within evolutionary history, and the action of God within the evolutionary process.

The next major step (chapter four) will be to ask: What does this story of the emerging universe have to do with Jesus? If this question is to be answered with care today it has to take into account the historical work on Jesus, the "new quest of the historical Jesus." As chapter two is an attempt to listen to what science says about the story of the cosmos, chapter four will be an attempt to listen to what historical research reveals about Jesus of Nazareth.

In chapter five I will bring this story of Jesus into relationship with three more principles from Rahner's theology. These principles concern the place of Jesus of Nazareth in the evolutionary history of the cosmos.

In the sixth chapter the focus of attention will turn to the future, to what theology calls eschatology. It will be necessary to listen, in very summary fashion, to what science has to say, this time not about the origin of things, but about the end of the Earth and the end of the universe.

Chapter seven will be an attempt to look at this same question from the theological perspective. Three principles of Rahner's theology will be brought forward as part of a dialogue with the insights of science.

In chapter eight the focus will be on the resurrected Christ. The question will be: What relationship is there between the risen Christ and the material universe? In this chapter I will be moving beyond the explicit systematic theology of Rahner, and taking his line of thought a little further.

The last chapter will bring together, in summary form, the theological principles outlined in the book, and discuss some of the consequences of this theological system for a contemporary practice.

NOTES

1. *The Advertiser* (31 August 1989) 6.
2. There is, of course, an enormous shift in the understanding of nature between the work of Newton and the work of Einstein and quantum theorists like Neils Bohr. For a study of the impact of this shift on theology see John Honner, "Nature, Physics and Theology Naturalized," *Compass* 21 (Summer 1987) 13–18. See also his *The Description of Nature: Neils Bohr and the Philosophy of Quantum Physics* (Oxford: Clarendon Press, 1987). On this whole area see N. Max Wildiers, *The Theologian and His Universe* (New York: Seabury Press, 1982). See also Louis

Bouyer, *Cosmos: The World and the Glory of God* (Petersham, Massachusetts: St. Bede's Publications, 1988).

3. Teilhard's great work on this theme was, of course, *The Phenomenon of Man* (London: William Collins, 1959).

4. See Thomas Berry, *The Dream of the Earth* (San Francisco: Sierra Club Books, 1988); Anne Lonergan and Caroline Richards (editors), *Thomas Berry and the New Cosmology* (Mystic: Twenty-Third Publications, 1987). On this theme see the important address of Joseph Sittler to the 1961 Assembly of the World Council of Churches, entitled "Called to Unity," *The Ecumenical Review* 14 (1961) pp. 181–90. See also H. Paul Santmire, *The Travail of Nature* (Philadelphia: Fortress Press, 1985).

5. Sean McDonagh, *To Care for the Earth: A Call to a New Theology* (Santa Fe: Bear and Company, 1986); *The Greening of the Church* (Scoresby, Victoria: Canterbury Press, 1990).

6. See Matthew Fox's *Original Blessing* (Santa Fe: Bear & Co., 1983); *The Coming of the Cosmic Christ* (Melbourne: Collins Dove, 1988).

7. Michael J. Himes and Kenneth Himes, "The Sacrament of Creation: Towards an Environmental Theology," *Commonweal* (January 26, 1990) 42–49. See also Tony Kelly's "Wholeness: Ecological and Catholic?" in *Pacifica* 3 (June, 1990) pp. 201–23.

8. Jurgen Moltmann, *God in Creation: An Ecological Doctrine of Creation* (London: SCM, 1985); Gabriel Daly, *Creation and Redemption* (Dublin: Gill and Macmillan, 1988). See also Ulrich Duchrow and Gerhard Liedke, *Shalom: Biblical Perspectives on Creation, Justice and Peace* (Geneva: WCC Publications, 1989). Moltmann's most recent work, *The Way of Christ Jesus* (London: SCM, 1990) is an important attempt at a systemic christology cast in the framework of creation. However, I find his critique of Rahner unconvincing. He does not take account of much of Rahner's work, particularly his theology of redemption, and of the "New Earth," and I find myself unable to accept the extreme dialectic Moltmann sets up between evolution and redemption.

9. Kathryn Tanner, *God and Creation in Christian Theology: Tyranny or Empowerment?* (Oxford: Basil Blackwell, 1988).

10. See Rosemary Radford Ruether, *Sexism and God-Talk: Towards a Feminist Theology* (London: SCM, 1983); Sallie McFague, *Mod-

els of God: Theology for an Ecological Nuclear Age (London: SCM, 1987). Sallie McFague develops the idea of the world as God's body, and presents models of God as Mother, Lover and Friend. For a helpful discussion of feminist contributions see Robert G. Simons, "The Impact of the Feminist Critique on Christology: Towards an Enhanced Cosmological Soteriology," *Compass* 23 (Summer 1989) 37–45. See also William M. Thompson, *The Jesus Debate* (New York: Paulist Press, 1985), particularly 419–427.

    11. A.R. Peacocke, *Creation and the World of Science: The Bampton Lectures, 1978* (Oxford: Clarendon Press, 1979); *God and the New Biology* (London: J.M. Dent, 1986). For a comparison of the work of Peacocke with that of Moltmann see the article by Jim McPherson, "The Integrity of Creation: Science, History, and Theology" in *Pacifica* 2 (1989) 333–355.

    12. Charles Birch and John B. Cobb, Jr., *The Liberation of Life: From the Cell to the Community* (Cambridge: Cambridge University Press, 1981). See also Charles Birch, *On Purpose* (Kensington: New South Wales University Press, 1990).

    13. John Polkinghorne, *One World: The Interaction of Science and Theology* (Princeton: Princeton University Press, 1986); *Science and Creation: The Search for Understanding* (London: SPCK, 1988).

    14. Daniel Liderbach, *The Numinous Universe* (New York: Paulist Press, 1989).

    15. Juan Luis Segundo, *An Evolutionary Approach to Jesus of Nazareth* (Maryknoll: Orbis Press, 1988).

2

The Story of the Cosmos— Matter, Life and Consciousness

The advances made by science during this last century have led to a radically new understanding of the universe, which has left the general public, and most theologians, well behind. It is good news, then, that a number of scientists have made serious attempts to communicate the new understanding of the universe to a wider public.[1]

A theology which hopes to make a serious response to the world of the late twentieth century must take this new scientific picture into account. While only the most fundamentalist of Christian theologians would consider themselves bound to the scientific worldview of the two creation accounts in the book of Genesis, most theologians have not grappled directly with the alternative worldview posed by modern science. There are reasons for this, of course, like the fact that there is no one worldview of science, and the fact that attempting to cross disciplines is a risky venture for the theologian, as it is for anyone else.

Nevertheless I believe that it is important to take this risk. In the pages that follow I will attempt to tell the story of the universe in the way that reflects the mainstream of modern science. I will not be able, of course, to discuss the frontiers of scientific discovery, nor to deal with many matters that are still highly speculative and controversial. The aim here is the modest one of presenting a broad overview that most scientists would find generally acceptable. This, then, will provide a perspective for contemporary theological reflection.

The Expanding Universe

We are learning to see the world in an entirely different way from our ancestors. Part of this new picture is the sheer size of the universe put before us by twentieth century science.

We now know that the Sun is one of more than two hundred thousand million stars that make up our galaxy, the Milky Way. This galaxy of ours is so wide that light, traveling at three hundred thousand kilometers a second, takes a hundred thousand years to cross it. Our Sun is a star of average size, situated about 27,000 light-years from the center of the galaxy, near the edge of one of the spiral arms.

The Sun, with its solar system, travels in a circular orbit around the galaxy at a speed of 210 kilometers per second. It takes about 250 million years for the Sun to rotate around the galaxy, and in its lifetime it has probably made this journey about 20 times. The size of the Milky Way is beyond imagination.

Yet we have come to know that there are many galaxies far larger than the Milky Way. It is sobering to remember that it was only in 1924 that the American astronomer Edwin Hubble demonstrated that our galaxy was not the only one in the universe. There are many others! Astronomers now tell us that the observable universe contains more than a hundred thousand million galaxies.

Edwin Hubble also investigated the fact that the spectral lines of the light coming from distant galaxies are shifted to the red. Their light is "red-shifted." This could be explained only by the fact that these stars are moving away from us. Because of the relationship between the frequency of light waves and the relative speed of the stars (the Doppler effect) light from stars moving toward us is blue-shifted, while light from those moving away is red-shifted. In 1929 Hubble published his findings which showed that most galaxies were moving away from us, and that the further away they are, the faster they are moving from us.

This meant that the universe could no longer be understood

as static. The distance between galaxies is growing all the time. We inhabit an expanding world. Stephen Hawking, who is a prominent theoretical physicist and the Lucasian Professor of Mathematics at Cambridge University, has said that "the discovery that the universe is expanding was one of the great intellectual revolutions of the twentieth century."[2]

The fact that the universe is expanding suggests that the expansion began from an extremely compressed and dense state. It supports the idea of an initial explosion. According to the most common scientific view, the universe had its beginning between 10,000 and 20,000 million years ago with a primeval explosion, known as the "big bang."

Science understands this explosion to be the origin not only of matter, but of space and time as well. Einstein's general theory of relativity argues that gravity is a distortion of both space and time. Time is inextricably linked to space. As space stretches so does time. The expanding universe is not seen as matter exploding through space, so much as space-time itself stretching and inflating.

The discovery in 1965 of background microwave radiation throughout the universe has lent further support to the big bang theory over "steady state" and other theories of the universe. It is believed that this microwave radiation survives from the radiation era of the big bang, so that scientists can describe the universe filled with this radiation as "bathed in the afterglow of the big bang."[3] The temperature of this cosmic afterglow, three degrees above absolute zero, is a remnant of the intense heat of the fiery origin of the universe.

Since the early 1970s particle accelerators have been able to simulate the heat of the initial explosion. Scientists have made detailed mathematical speculations about events that occurred in the first fraction of a second of the universe's existence.[4] The cosmologist Edward Harrison says that "everything happens with such rapidity in the very early universe that perhaps more of cosmic history occurs in the first thousandth of a second than has occurred in ten billion years since."[5]

Within the first second the temperature would have been so high that ordinary atomic nuclei could not have existed. In its early stage, the exploding universe consisted of a mixture of individual subatomic particles, protons, neutrons, electrons, photons and neutrinos, whirling about in chaotic fashion. It can be estimated that within the first few minutes, as the universe expanded and cooled down to below a billion degrees, about 25 percent of the original atomic material would form into nuclei of helium (with a slight amount of deuterium, and even smaller amounts of lithium and carbon) and the remaining 75 percent would remain in the form of protons, destined to become hydrogen. The fact that the universe today is made up of about 25 percent helium and 75 percent hydrogen gives further support to the big bang theory of origin.

The original explosion occurred with exactly the right balance of expansive force and gravitation. Had the force of the explosion been weaker, then the expanding universe would have fallen back in upon itself. Had it been a fraction stronger, the cosmic matter would have flown apart so rapidly that galaxies could never have formed.[6]

Eventually, the great hydrogen clouds of the exploding universe began to coalesce, and fall in upon themselves under the pull of gravitation, and the long process of formation of galaxies began. As temperatures rose because of gravitational forces, nuclear reactions ignited at the core of the nebulas, fueled by the conversion of hydrogen into helium. The first stars were born.

About 5,000 million years ago our solar system had its origins as a huge cloud of primordial material. This "parent nebula" was made up of swirling particles of dust and gas. It began to shrink as a result of gravitational forces. Density and temperature increased in the center of the nebula. Gravitational pressure eventually ignited the thermonuclear action of the Protosun. Rings of matter spun off from the nebula formed in individual units around the Sun, and their own forces of gravitation began to mold them into the spherical planets we know.

Life on Earth

The emerging planet Earth was bombarded with meteorites, formed from the original cosmic dust. The process was one of accretion, as larger bodies and smaller particles were pulled together by gravitational forces.

Earth took its position at exactly the right distance from the Sun to enable it, in due course, to support life. The interior heated under gravitational pressure, and formed a molten core. Heavy metal sank to the center, and lighter materials rose toward the top, eventually forming a crust. This crust enclosed a mantle, which in turn surrounded the core. Both the continental crusts and the oceanic crusts are now understood to ride on rigid plates (lithospheric plates) which move on a plastic layer called the asthenosphere.

Some rocks have been dated as 3,600 million years old, although most are younger than this. The planet itself is thought to be about 4,600 million years old. This is quite a shift from earlier estimates. In seventeenth century Europe, for example, the Earth was thought to be 4,000 years old.

In the process of separation between the molten core and the rest of the planet a large amount of gas was released. As the earth cooled an initial atmosphere emerged. Probably this did not contain free oxygen.

The formation of Earth's water cycle (the hydrosphere) has also been understood to be largely a by-product of the separation of the Earth's mantle and the crust. It was thought that water came from within the Earth. More recent studies of the impact of meteorites and asteroids on the moon, in the period of 4,500 to

3,300 million years ago, have led scientists to argue that this period of intense bombardment by ice-bearing meteorites may have been highly significant in the formation of the Earth's oceans. It seems that "an extraterrestrial source for a significant fraction of the Earth's oceans can no longer be rejected."[7]

Scientists believe that it was in the oceans, the tidal pools and the estuaries that the mysterious chemical changes took place that allowed the development of the first forms of life. In a famous experiment at the University of Chicago in 1952, Stanley Miller and Harold Urey attempted to simulate conditions on Earth 3,000 million years ago. They passed an electric charge (substituting for lightning) through a mixture of hydrogen, methane and ammonia gases, and boiling water. After a week they found that the brown liquid that formed contained some organic compounds which are basic to life, including amino acids. This experiment, important as it is, does not yet go near to explaining the emergence of complex molecules like the awesome DNA.[8]

The fossil record indicates the presence of life on Earth in the form of blue-green bacteria (cyanobacteria) in the early Precambrian period. The oldest rocks known to contain the remains of living cells, in the form of blue-green algae, have been found at Warrawoona in Australia. They are thought to be 3,500 million years old. Perhaps these minute bacterial organisms were the main form of life on the planet for the next 2,500 million years.

From the study of the chemistry of rocks it seems that oxygen in the Earth's atmosphere made its appearance in the same period as the blue-green bacteria. Apparently oxygen appeared as a result of photosynthesis in blue-green bacteria and other early life forms. Continued photosynthesis meant that the amount of oxygen in the atmosphere could be maintained at about twenty-one percent. This allowed a rich life system to emerge.

The first fossils we have of any kind of animal life are of marine invertebrates. They come from the end of the Precambrian period (between 600 and 700 million years ago). From the Palaeozoic period (between 570 and 230 million years ago) there are a great number of fossils: in the middle of this period we find fish with skeletons, and, toward its end, various forms of bony fish, sharks and rays.

About 400 million years ago the first forms of simple vascular plants appeared on land, and from the later part of the Palaezoic period there is the first evidence of vertebrates on land, in the form of fishlike amphibians. By the end of the Palaezoic period the first reptiles appear in the fossil record.

Reptiles were to dominate the Earth during the next great period, the Mesozoic, between 230 and 65 million years ago. It was during this age of the dinosaurs that warm-blooded mammals first made their appearance. Toward the end of this period we find the first fossils of birds and flowering plants.

With the disappearance of the dinosaurs, mammals were able to take center-stage and to spread into various regions. Their ability to regulate their temperature meant that they could colonize areas with differing climates, including the great forests. In the Cenozoic period, which began 65 million years ago, a wide variety of species emerged. At the start of this period the first primates appeared.

The Emergence of Human Life

In Africa palaeontologists have discovered fossils of human-like creatures that have been called *Australopithecus.* They seem to have lived from about four million to one million years ago, and although they had a relatively small brain cavity, they stood erect.

More closely related to modern men and women is the group described as *Homo erectus.* They lived during a period which lasted from about 2 million years ago until about 259 thousand years ago. They migrated from Africa to Asia and Europe. *Homo erectus* had a larger cranium than *Australopithecus,* and used fire and tools.

We know about an early form of *Homo sapiens,* the Nean-
derthal subspecies, from discoveries of bones and artifacts in
various European locations. The best examples of these are between seventy and forty thousand years old, but it is thought that
Neanderthals may have evolved "from an archaic form of *Homo
sapiens* perhaps as much as 200,000 years ago."[9]

Evidence of modern humankind (*Homo sapiens sapiens*),
with a very large brain and small face and teeth, comes from
various places at about the same time. Anthropologists suggest
that it is likely that "far-flung populations reached this stage of
evolutionary progress at roughly the same time—between 30,000
and 40,000 years ago."[10]

However, recent discoveries of human artifacts on the Ne-
pean River near Sydney have been dated as up to 47,000 years old.
These tools are assumed to be artifacts of *homo sapiens sapiens,*
and it is also assumed that the toolmakers were ancestral to modern Aboriginal people.[11] The current evidence has modern humankind in Australia between 43,000 and 47,000 years ago, in
Europe about 35,000 years ago, in Africa about 32,000 years ago,
and in the Americas less than 20,000 years ago.

Somewhere in this process of the emergence of *homo sapiens,*
at a point we cannot pin down with the present evidence, human
self-consciousness emerged. Human beings gathered in tribal soci-
eties on all the continents and developed communal cultures and
spiritualities that were often in close relationship with the Earth.
Complex civilizations emerged in Mesopotamia, Egypt, Greece,
India, China, and among the Mayans and Aztecs.

At the end of the twentieth century we look back on a recent
history of European expansion and colonization of much of the
world, the industrial revolution, a rapid increase in scientific understanding, and the extraordinary development of human techno-
logical capacity.

Twentieth century technology has made it much easier for
human beings to become conscious that they inhabit one common

world. Yet global solidarity is far from realized. Poverty, starvation and malnutrition afflict many of Earth's citizens. Wealth is maintained in the hands of the rich nations by an international economic order, and a system of borrowing and debt, which means that poorer countries are depleting their natural resources in a losing battle to service their debts.

Since the first atomic bomb was dropped on Hiroshima on August 6, 1945, the world has lived in fear of nuclear destruction. However, as the twentieth century comes toward its end, human beings have come to see that the pollution of land, sea and atmosphere constitutes an even greater threat to the future of the planet.

This state of affairs is entirely new. The industrial age has been in existence for less than 200 years. When we reflect about the level of damage done to a system that has been 5,000 million years in the making, we are forced to rethink our whole approach to life on Earth.

What is exciting and full of promise is that many of Earth's inhabitants are reflecting on these issues, and are committing themselves to a new global solidarity. This opens up new possibilities for a new economics directed toward the well-being of every human person, and the well-being of the planet itself, built upon the premise of respect for every species on the planet. It gives some reason for the hope that humankind will be able to make a fundamental option to care for the Earth.

NOTES

1. See, for example, Bernard Lovell, *In the Centre of Immensities* (London: Hutchinson and Co., 1978), and John Barrow and Joseph Silk, *The Left Hand of Creation* (Basic Books: New York, 1983). A significant example of a modern scientist reaching out to the general public is

Stephen Hawking in his *A Brief History of Time: From the Big Bang to Black Holes* (London: Bantam Press, 1988). Another is Ilya Prigogine. In their introduction to *Order Out of Chaos* (London: Heinemann, 1984), Ilya Prigogine and Isabelle Stengers write: "We must open new channels of communication between science and society. It is in this spirit that this book has been written" (p. 22). Paul Davies has written widely and clearly on recent developments in science. See, for example, his *God and the New Physics* (London: Penguin Books, 1983); *Superforce* (London: Heinemann, 1984); *The Cosmic Blueprint* (London: Unwin, 1987).

2. Stephen Hawking, *A Brief History of Time*, 39.

3. Edward Harrison, *Cosmology: The Science of the Universe* (Cambridge: Cambridge University Press, 1981) 347. See also Robert Wagoner and Donald Goldsmith, *Cosmic Horizons: Understanding the Universe* (San Francisco: W.H. Freeman and Company, 1982); Jayant Narlikar, *The Structure of the Universe* (Oxford: Oxford University Press, 1977).

4. For an account of this see Steven Weinberg, *The First Three Minutes* (London: Deutsch, 1977), and John Gribbin, *In Search of the Big Bang* (London: Corgi Books, 1986). For more recent discussion of the origin of the universe, particularly the idea that the universe, although finite, has no boundary or edge, see Stephen Hawking, *A Brief History of Time*.

5. Edward R. Harrison, *Cosmology: The Science of the Universe*, 354.

6. Paul Davies writes: "At the so-called Planck time (10^{-43} seconds) (which is the earliest moment at which the concept of space and time has meaning) the matching was accurate to a staggering one part in 10^{60}. That is to say, had the explosion differed in strength at the outset by only one part in 10^{60}, the universe we now perceive would not exist. To give some meaning to these numbers, suppose you wanted to fire a bullet at a one-inch target on the other side of the observable universe, twenty billion light years away. Your aim would have to be accurate to that same part in 10^{60}" (*God and the New Physics*, 179). Davies goes on to point out that a possible explanation for the balance of forces in the expanding universe can be found in the concept of the "inflationary universe" introduced by Alan Guth. See also John Polkinghorne, *One World: The Interaction of Science and Theology*, 57.

7. This is the conclusion of Christopher F. Chyba, in his "The Cometary Contributions to the Oceans of Primitive Earth," *Nature* 330 (1987) 634. See also his article "Impact Delivery and Erosion of Planetary Oceans in the Early Inner Solar System," in *Nature* 343 (1990) 129–133.

8. For a helpful treatment of current thinking on the origin of life see Arthur Peacocke, *God and the New Biology,* particularly 133–160. In *The Cosmic Blueprint* (p. 118) Paul Davies states that "the spontaneous generation of life by random shuffling is a ludicrously improbable event." It is less probable than the chances of flipping heads on a coin six million times in a row. Davies recognizes the need to postulate some kind of principle of self-organization at the origin of life, in line with the work of Prigogine and Eigen.

9. David Lambert, *The Cambridge Guide to Prehistoric Man* (Cambridge: Cambridge University Press, 1987) 138.

10. Sharon S. and Thomas McKern, *Tracking Fossil Man* (New York: Praeger Publishers, 1970) 125.

11. See the article by Eugene Stockton "Their Blackened Stump Is Holy Seed," *Compass* 22 (Autumn/Winter 1988) 19–25.

3

A Theological Reading of the Story of the Universe

> Wisdom, the fashioner of all things, taught me. For in her
> there is a spirit that is intelligent, holy, unique, manifold,
> subtle, mobile, clear, unpolluted, distinct, invulnerable, lov-
> ing the good, keen, irresistible, beneficent, humane, steadfast,
> sure, free from anxiety, all-powerful, overseeing all, and pen-
> etrating through all spirits that are intelligent and pure and
> most subtle. For wisdom is more mobile than any motion;
> because of her pureness she pervades and penetrates all
> things. For she is a breath of the power of God, and a pure
> emanation of the glory of the Almighty (Wis 7:22–26).

The story of the universe told in the preceding section is
meant to be a reasonably accurate summary of the picture that
emerges from contemporary physics, astronomy, geology,
palaeontology and biology. Of course there are many differences
between scientists about details, and there are major disagree-
ments in their theoretical explanations for the origin of the universe, life and consciousness. Nevertheless, I think it can be said
that the story told above reflects a broad scientific consensus.

How does theology deal with this story? Karl Rahner offers
some helpful insights, which can be creative points of dialogue
between theology and the scientific story of the universe. In this
chapter I will discuss three of these insights: first, that all creatures form one community grounded in their creator; second, that
human beings are the cosmos come to self-awareness before God;
third, that evolutionary change is empowered by the pressure of
the divine being from within creatures.

The Community of All Creatures in God

One of the most important theological truths concerning creation is simply that creation is one. This fundamental truth has often been forgotten within Christianity where the tendency toward dualism has done enormous harm. Of course Christianity has resisted the extreme dualism of movements like Gnosticism and Manicheism. Nevertheless, early Christian thinkers, intent upon communicating the gospel within a Greek culture, naturally made use of current philosophical assumptions which were, in part, derived from Plato's thought.

This Neoplatonic culture exulted in what it saw as the higher, spiritual world of ideas, and tended to despise the material world accessible to the senses. Through the theology of the great thinkers of the early church like Augustine, strands of Neoplatonic philosophy have influenced the whole subsequent tradition. At times Christianity has been seduced from within by various forms of Neoplatonic dualism.

The world of nature has been set over against human culture, the country over against the city, the body over against the spirit, feelings over against thinking, the female over against the male, what is human over against the divine. Dualistic thinking sets up polarities and then presents one side of a polarity (like the spirit) as worthy and free and related to the divine, and the other side of the polarity (like the body) as demeaning, enslaving and demonic.

Dualistic thinking tends to be suspicious of bodiliness, relationship to matter, connection with the fertility of nature, feelings, instincts, the unconscious and women. Because of the priority it gives to the world of ideas it has tended to be suspicious and repressive toward a science centered on the observable and the material. Within Christianity, it appears in fundamentalist theologies and in spiritualities which encourage a "flight from the world" as a prerequisite for union with God.

Dualism is bad theology, as is its opposite, the collapsing of all differences and the refusal to see the complexity of things, which is sometimes called monism. The problem with dualism is that while it does not deny complexity, it seeks to manage it by elevating one dimension of life to the level of the divine, and reducing the other side to nothing, or to the demonic.

Rahner's answer, and that of many other theologians, is to see the totality of creation, with all its immense diversity, as part of a unified whole. The only adequate theological response to our complex world is holistic thinking. This theological holism is firmly grounded in the one creator God. This can be spelled out in three inter-related statements: first, it is the one God who creates the whole cosmos as one diverse but inter-related system; second, this same creator is present to every part of the cosmos sustaining and empowering it; third, this same God will bring the whole movement of evolving creation to its completion.[1]

The abundance and immense variety of creation forms a unified whole. Creation is one world, united in its origin, its self-realization and its goal. There is an inner similarity and inter-relationship of all creatures.

In this community of all creation each species has its own unique place. Every creature bears the "stamp of origin" of the creator, the one primordial ground of all being.[2] Every type of creature, then, must be understood as reflecting something of the mystery of the creator. Humankind is part of a world of beings which are all related to one another as one community grounded in the life of God.

A key issue here is the relationship between matter and spirit. So often human beings have been unable to resist the temptation to see their bodies as connected to the Earth and the rest of creation, and to see their spirits or souls as soaring into a pure world beyond the bonds of matter. Naturally this has led to a devaluing of the body and of Earth itself.

Matter and spirit cannot be divided in this way. They are

radically interconnected in the community of creation. According to Karl Rahner matter and spirit must be seen as having more uniting them than dividing them. Their inter-relationship can be grasped properly only by reflecting on our own experience of both these dimensions within ourselves. We experience matter and spirit as two related dimensions of our one human existence. The human person forms a unity which is prior to any divisions or distinctions between matter and spirit.

What is matter? Matter is that side of ourselves and others which we experience as specific, concrete and bodily. We experience both ourselves and the world around us as matter insofar as both our own selves and the world around us appear to us as factual realities, with their own proper and independent existence. It is because we are matter that we can truly encounter others. Because of matter there is the possibility of communication and love between free human beings. Matter accounts for the otherness of human beings to themselves and to each other. Matter is the necessary condition for becoming conscious of oneself, and of the mystery that encompasses life.

Spirit is simply the human person insofar as this person becomes conscious of self in an absolute way. Rahner argues that whenever we become conscious of other beings in the world, and become conscious of ourselves, we are also aware, at least in a preconceptual way, of the limitless mystery of being. Our self-consciousness occurs by the very fact that we differentiate ourselves against the "absoluteness of reality as such and towards its one ground which we call God."[3] Spirit is the human person insofar as he or she is conscious of self, and also necessarily conscious, in some way, of the mystery that surrounds our life in the world. It is in the free and loving acceptance of this mystery that the human person is most radically spirit.

Matter and spirit are two related elements of the one human person. There is an essential difference between them and they cannot be reduced to each other, but neither can they be separated. Only when both are considered do our eyes remain open to all the dimensions of the human person.

Matter and spirit make up one world. They share one common history, in which matter has evolved toward spirit, or consciousness. After all, the creator of matter is the absolute spirit, who can hardly be thought of as creating something entirely unrelated to spirit. Matter comes from spirit and is oriented toward spirit. Rahner argues that it is intrinsic to matter that it develops toward spirit. According to him, matter develops "out of its own inner being in the directions of spirit."[4] He maintains that "the development of biologically organized materiality is orientated in terms of an ever-increasing complexity and interiority towards spirit, until finally, under the dynamic impulse of God's creative power, and through a process of self-transcendence of this kind, it becomes spirit."[5]

The material world is radically and fundamentally one. This is why theology has been able to understand the whole of reality as touched to its very roots by the incarnation. This is why a theologian like Rahner can see the created universe as what happens when God wants to communicate in love with the non-divine: the material world is the "addressee" and the recipient of God's self-utterance.[6]

We human beings, with our ability to think and reflect, our self-consciousness, our capacity for communication and love, and our creativity in art and science, are intimately bonded in a relationship of mutual interdependence with all living creatures on this planet. We are related to the whole great world of matter. We are part of it all, from the giant supernova out in space to the tiny electron responding mysteriously to the presence of the human observer in a laboratory, from the great whales of the oceans to the smallest insects of a rain forest.

Human Beings as the Cosmos
Come to Self-Consciousness

Can we say any more about the relationship between human beings and other creatures? How are we to understand the place of the human person in the evolving cosmos?

The uncritical view that everything revolves around human beings, and is at their disposal, has led to disastrous results. It was this kind of thinking, generally called anthropocentrism, that was responsible for the brutal opposition to Copernicus, Giordano Bruno and Galileo, and to their demonstration that human beings are not at the center of the universe.

In more recent times, individuals, corporations and states have used this anthropocentric tradition to justify ripping the rain forests from the Earth, polluting the atmosphere and the seas, and annihilating countless species. In the light of this, it is not surprising that the anthropocentric approach comes in for a good deal of criticism from both scientists and ecologists.

The alternative view, often put forward in an unsystematic way, suggests that human beings are simply one species among many others, and they have no more dignity or rights than any other creature. This "leveling" view, which is currently very popular, ends up in untenable positions. Where it is adopted uncritically a human person can be understood to have no more value than a worm, or a fungus. It tends to remove the moral imperative which gives priority to the oppressed poor of the Earth, and so runs the risk of isolating ecological concerns from concern for social justice.

What is needed is a way of seeing the human person which avoids both a mindless anthropocentrism and the undermining of human dignity. I believe that Rahner's theological concept can help to mediate between these extremes. He suggests that the human person can be understood as the cosmos come to conscious-ness of itself.[7] He argues that it is of the very nature of the material universe to develop toward consciousness. Human beings are part of the cosmos, part of one single history of evolution. Within this one history human beings are the cosmos come to self-awareness. The material universe finds itself in them. As will become clear later in this book, this does not mean that there are no other intelligent and self-conscious beings in the universe. There may well be extraterrestrial beings who are also the cosmos come to self-consciousness.

Rahner is not the only writer to develop the line of thought that human beings are the universe come to self-awareness. Teil-hard de Chardin had already described human beings as discover-ing that they were "nothing else than evolution become conscious of itself." Moreover Teilhard acknowledged that he had borrowed this expression from Julian Huxley.[8] A number of contemporary writers on science use similar expressions. Carl Sagan, for exam-ple, writes that we human beings are "the local embodiment of a Cosmos grown to self-awareness."[9] Arthur Peacocke states that "in human beings part of the world has become conscious of itself and consciously and actively responds to its surroundings." In another context he says that in humanity "matter has become aware of itself, of its past, and of its unfulfilled potentialities."[10] Paul Davies writes that in human beings "the universe has orga-nized its own self-awareness."[11] According to Thomas Berry hu-man beings appear as "the moment in which the unfolding uni-verse becomes conscious of itself." We carry the universe in our being as the universe carries us in its being—"the two have a total presence to each other and to that deeper mystery out of which both the universe and ourselves have emerged."[12]

In Rahner this proposition is taken with utmost seriousness as a theological statement, a statement about God. God has made matter in such a way that it becomes self-aware and capable of entering into a free and personal relationship with God. This gives a new perspective, and new depth, to the relationship that human beings have with all of matter, to every giant galaxy thousands of millions of light years away, and to every subatomic particle. Human beings are all of this come to awareness of itself.

Human community and the increased level of communication between the peoples of the Earth are part of the one story of the cosmos.[13] The unfolding of the universe continues in the human person and in human community. It is manifest in growing global solidarity, in culture, and in human interaction with the rest of creation.

But the movement of self-transcendence at the heart of cosmic processes does not reach its fulfillment simply in human life, or in human community, but only in the embrace between creator and creatures that is called grace. The evolutionary history of the cosmos reaches its climax only when the creative Ground of the whole cosmic process engages in self-giving love with the free human person.

We live in a world of grace, a world in which God is present in self-offering to human beings at every point. Every act of knowing, every free act, is an opening toward the mystery that comes close to us in love. The experience of wonder at the universe, the experience of human limitation, the experience of friendship, the experience of solitude, the experience of loss and death, the experience of the sheer bounty of life—these and many other experiences open women and men to the mystery at the heart of human existence.

Christian revelation tells us that this experience of mystery can be identified as God present, reaching out toward us in self-offering. Our existence is encompassed by grace, which is nothing other than the presence of God, freely turned toward us in self-offering. Grace is the heartbeat of the universe. It is God bent over us in love. The life of faith is simply the free response to this love, directed toward us from every point of the universe.

The goal of the cosmic process of self-transcendence is immediacy between creation and creator, experienced in God's free self-communication to spiritual creatures and through them to the whole cosmos. As individual persons, we experience only the beginnings of the movement toward our infinite goal. This experience of grace in our lives gives us hope of a future glory which will be the fulfillment of human and cosmic life. It gives us grounds for hope "in the fulfillment of the coming history of the cosmos and of each individual cosmic consciousness, which consists in the direct experience of God."[14]

Of course this process whereby the universe comes to self-awareness happens only in a partial way in any one person. Rahner notes that the process can seem tentative and it can appear to fail. Nevertheless, every human person, through his or her bodiliness, is always an element of the cosmos, and cannot be cut off from the cosmos. Through each member of the human community, the cosmos presses forward toward self-consciousness. Rahner can say that "the one material cosmos is the single body as it were of a multiple self-presence of this very cosmos and its orientation towards its absolute and infinite ground."[15]

Obviously, this position differs from "leveling" views of the place of humans in the universe since it sees human beings, and their self-transcendence toward God, as the goal of the evolutionary process. It gives humankind and every human being enormous dignity. At the same time it differs from traditional anthropocentrism because it is profoundly relational. It views human beings as intimately related to the Earth and as "companions" to every other creature.[16]

The story of the cosmos and the story of humankind are a single story. The evolutionary history of the cosmos involves not only the movement from matter to life, and the movement from life to self-consciousness, but also the experience by conscious and free persons of God's self-communication by grace. If human beings are the cosmos come to consciousness before the grace of God, if they are the self-transcendence of matter, they remain profoundly interconnected with birds, rain forests, insects, photosynthesis, quantum particles and the Milky Way.

God—The Dynamic Impulse from Within Creatures

If man and woman are in fact the evolving universe become aware of itself, then we face a fundamental question: How are we to understand this whole evolutionary movement? How can we account for the transition from inert matter to life? How can we explain the emergence of a human world?

Some scientists would argue that we must seek answers to these and similar questions by continuing to follow the classical method, which has studied the universe by reducing it to its smallest parts. These "reductionists" would focus attention only on the behavior of molecular and atomic particles. A number of them, like the French biologist Jacques Monod, argue that the universe unfolds simply through the random interplay of chance and necessity. He writes: "Pure chance, absolutely free but blind, is at the very root of the stupendous edifice of evolution."[17]

Other scientists, sometimes called the "holist" school, argue for the need to look at the larger picture in order to account for nature's ability to order the universe. Some who take this position insist that the two methods, reductionism and holism, operate at different levels, and that, far from being antagonistic to one another, they are both necessary. One who holds this view is the physicist Paul Davies.[18]

Davies is one of many scientists convinced that there are self-organizing principles at work in nature. At the end of the twentieth century they are presenting us with a new and exciting scientific paradigm—the self-organizing universe. Science has long accepted the general idea of the dissipation of usable energy, in the concept of entropy and the famous second law of thermodynamics.[19] Without contradicting this law, it is clear that there is also, at certain points within the universe and its processes, a concentration of energy which builds things up. Through the work of researchers like Ilya Prigogine on far-from-equilibrium systems, we are now coming to understand how open systems can increase in order and complexity.[20]

This work may lead to new scientific principles concerned with the cooperative qualities of complex systems, which will help us understand evolutionary progress in the universe.[21] Recent discoveries in the study of systems which exhibit chaotic behavior, and new approaches in many fields, including biology, physics, chemistry, astronomy and neurology, show a tendency toward complexity, organization and order at work in nature.[22] Davies discusses this research from quite different specialities, and he shows how it indicates that there is, in our universe, both a widespread tendency toward self-organization, and a capacity to cross critical thresholds into new stages of complexity.

These abrupt transitions to new states of complexity cannot be explained simply by the "random shuffling" of atomic particles or molecules. New approaches in research are aimed at discovering what it is that enables systems to move to complex and organized states. Such research may allow us to understand more about the process of self-organization by which systems "suddenly and spontaneously leap into elaborate forms," which are characterized "by greater complexity, by cooperative behavior and global coherence."[23]

In the 1970s James Lovelock introduced the concept of *Gaia* into cosmology.[24] He offered the hypothesis that the whole planet should be seen as one self-sustaining system of life, which he named *Gaia* after the Greek Earth goddess. *Gaia* is a way of thinking about the Earth as a holistic organism, an organism which itself shapes the land, the atmosphere and the oceans in such a way as to make them suitable to sustain life.

An example of this system at work is the regulation of the Earth's temperature. Over the Earth's history the sun's luminosity has increased by about 30 percent, because of the way its structure alters as it burns up hydrogen. Yet the temperature on the Earth has remained relatively constant, allowing life to emerge and survive. At the same time as the sun grew hotter, the carbon dioxide "blanket" around the Earth began to dissipate because of photosynthesis in the earliest forms of plant life. The result was that the Earth's temperature remained constant enough to allow life to continue and to develop on the planet. This maintenance of temperature is one of many examples of self-regulation by the life systems of the planet.

The *Gaia* hypothesis states that "the temperature, oxidation state, acidity, and certain aspects of the rocks and water are at any time kept constant, and this homoeostasis is maintained by active feedback processes operated automatically and unconsciously by the biota."[25] The atmosphere, the oceans, the climate and the crust are maintained at a state which is comfortable for life because of the behavior of living organisms.

Scientists have mixed reactions to *Gaia*. Some welcome the insight. Others dislike the mixture of scientific fact and mythic story, and question Lovelock's anthropomorphic approach to the biosphere. Nevertheless, the *Gaia* hypothesis raises important questions concerning the universe's capacity for self-organization.

What does theology have to say to all of this? What does the process of self-organization at the heart of the cosmos have to do with the Christian doctrine of God's creation of the whole universe?

First of all it is important to note that a theological explanation in no way replaces a scientific explanation. Science and theology each has its own distinct methodology. Science seeks an explanation of the universe through examining the elements of the universe and their interaction. Theology asks about the relationship between this world of beings revealed by science and the ground of being. It calls this ground of being God, and understands this God to be, by definition, inaccessible to the methods of natural science. Theology seeks to understand what science reveals from another, larger perspective. This perspective is quite rightly bracketed out in the method of scientific research.

There can be no question, then, of solving scientific problems by suddenly bringing in a theological reality. The task of theology is to look at the facts revealed by science and to ponder the mystery at the heart of them in the light of Christian faith. The biblical story of creation is not in competition with the scientific story, but a revelation capable of giving profound meaning to scientific discoveries.

Christian theology has the task of reflecting on the story of the universe told by contemporary science, including the big bang, the formation of galaxies, the development of our solar system, the first nuclear reaction of the Sun, the formation of the Earth's crust, the emergence of life in the form of blue-green algae, photosynthesis, the formation of a breathable atmosphere, the advent of animal life in the oceans and eventually on land, the period of the great reptiles and the first mammals, the emergence of the primates and the arrival of human beings. It would want to say that this unfolding of the cosmos is sustained and upheld by a mysterious being who escapes our comprehension, yet is engaged with us in a love which defies description.

This God who is at work in the becoming of the universe is drawing the world toward a future which is both unpredictable, and a fulfillment beyond all hopes. The openness of the cosmos to what is new, its capacity to leap forward across thresholds, its size and beauty, its sheer abundance, the stunning reality of planetary life, the emergence of intelligent beings capable of love and community—all of these direct the believer to the nature of the divine presence empowering the whole cosmic process.

But how are we to think more precisely about God's involvement with the evolving universe? Do we imagine God starting the process and then standing back like some great clock-maker? Or do we imagine God intervening from outside at certain points, like the first moment of life on Earth, or the existence of the first human being, to carry creation across the great thresholds to new possibilities?

Rahner suggests an alternative idea which can make sense within a scientific framework, and which is faithful to the Christian idea of the creator. His starting point is the profound theology of creation of Thomas Aquinas. For Aquinas creation is not simply an act of God at the beginning but rather a continuous engagement. God is the cause of all being without exception, which means that God creates, in a most radical sense, out of nothing.[26] According to Aquinas, creation is fundamentally and essentially a relationship. Creatures do not have within themselves the reason for their own existence. They are contingent beings—creatures who need not exist, who cannot account for their own being. They exist because of the absolute being of God. God *is* being. Creatures have being as a participation in God's absolute being.

According to Thomas Aquinas, then, creation is "the relation of the creature to the Creator as the principle of its very being."[27] In this view not only is God understood as holding all creatures in being (*conservatio*), but also as a principle cooperating in all their activities (*concursus*). God is understood as the absolute or primary cause of all things. This absolute causality of God's being does not cut across secondary causality whereby creatures have an effect upon one another.[28] By definition, it is the world of secondary causality that is accessible to the methods of science.

Rahner follows Aquinas closely in regarding creation as fundamentally a relationship between God's absolute being and the finite being of creatures, whereby finite beings are continuously constituted in existence by God. Creation is "not something that happens at the beginning of time, but is rather the continuing relationship of the world to its transcendent ground."[29] Creation is continuous. When Christians speak of creation at the beginning of time, what is really meant is that time itself is created, that God's creative act, which is itself eternal and identical with God, establishes a temporal world.

The understanding of creation developed by thinkers like Aquinas assumed a static view of the world. Rahner's contribution has been to rethink the issue of God's involvement with the world from an evolutionary worldview. What does it mean to speak of God's absolute being holding creatures in existence when we know that our Earth is a tiny part of the expanding universe, and that human beings are part of a chain of life which began with blue-green algae 3,500 million years ago?

What Rahner does is to take further the idea of God as the absolute being who conserves all creatures in being and cooperates in all their activities, and to understand God as the dynamic power which enables evolutionary change to occur. Creation is understood, now, not as a relationship between the absolute being of God and a static world, but as a relationship between the dynamic being of God and a world in process of coming to be. The traditional view of God's immanence as conserving and maintaining the abiding order of being becomes in Rahner's theology "the immanence of the divine dynamism in the world as a becoming."[30]

In the history of evolution, creatures become more than they were. Inert matter becomes a living organism. Living beings become conscious of themselves. If matter develops toward life, and life toward self-consciousness, then we are talking about a process whereby a reality becomes not just more than it was, but essentially different. The new dimension cannot simply be due to the creature in itself. It has become something it was not.

Of course this "more" could be explained through an extrinsic addition to what is there. For example, God could intervene from outside the system. But this fits neither with the scientific understanding of evolution nor with the normal theological understanding of the way God acts in relationship to creatures.[31]

Rahner suggests that evolutionary change occurs because of a power that comes from within the creature, but that this power is not due to the nature of the creature, but must be understood as the "pressure" of the divine being acting from within. This is the notion which he calls "active self-transcendence."[32]

It is not as if, in evolutionary change, a creature simply receives a new development from God "passively." Rather, the creature is itself empowered to an "active" self-transcendence. God is at the heart of evolutionary change as a power which enables the creature to go beyond itself and become more than it was. There are, then, two aspects to this concept, corresponding to the two parts of the expression "self-transcendence."

In the first place, the word "self" in the expression is meant to signify that the evolutionary shifts occur through a power which is truly intrinsic to the creature. The capacity of creation to go beyond itself and become more than it was comes from within creation itself. In the second place the word "transcendence" insists that this inner power does not belong to the being of the creature, but to the fullness of being, to God.

God is at the heart of the evolutionary process, empowering it from within. As Rahner says, "what was formerly understood by the terms '*conservatio*' and '*concursus*' in Christian theology is nothing else than the dynamic impulse towards precisely this self-transcendence present in all being in virtue of the immanence of God."[33]

Traditional theology never needed to explain how the cosmos might develop to the point of producing from within what are essentially new realities like life and consciousness. In this new theology the universe is understood to be a dynamic system. It is creative. It is self-organizing. Nature is understood to have within itself the creative ability to shape the universe. Evolutionary change comes about from within the cosmic process itself. It is up to science to study and explain the mechanisms of evolution. Theology affirms that what enables a creature to be what it is, and enables it to become more than it is in itself, is the power of active self-transcendence, which is the pressure of the divine being acting upon creation from within.

This divine reality cannot be discerned by natural science. The creative action of the divine being never supplants the creature, but cooperates at every point with the nature of each created being.

Evolutionary change is empowered by the dynamic presence of the absolute being of God. Evolutionary change occurs because of the presence of transforming love, which continually draws creation to a surprising and radically new future from within.

NOTES

1. See Rahner's *Foundations of Christian Faith* (New York: Seabury Press, 1978) 181–183; "Christology within an Evolutionary View of the World," in *Theological Investigations 5* (London: Darton, Longman and Todd, 1966; New York: Seabury Press, 1975), hence *T.I.*, 161–163.

2. See Rahner's "Natural Science and Reasonable Faith," *T.I.21*, 34.

3. *Foundations of Christian Faith*, 183. See also "Christology Within an Evolutionary View . . . ," 162–163. For a more developed treatment of the relationship between matter and spirit see "The Unity of Matter and Spirit in the Christian Understanding of Faith," *T.I.6*, 153–157.

4. "Christology Within an Evolutionary View . . . ," 164.

5. "Christology in the Setting . . . ," 218.

6. *Ibid.* 220.

7. See Rahner's *Foundations of Christian Faith*, 188–189. For a critique of Christian anthropocentrism see the famous article by Lynn White Jr., "The Historical Roots of Our Ecological Crisis," *Science* 155 (March 10, 1967) pp. 1203–7. While some of the critiques of Christianity fail to do justice to historical complexities there is no doubt that we

Christians need to come to terms with our past, and contribute from within our own heritage to a new ecological approach to life on Earth.

8. Teilhard de Chardin, *The Phenomenon of Man*, 243.

9. Carl Sagan, *Cosmos* (New York: Ballantine Books, 1980) 286.

10. Arthur Peacocke, *God and the New Biology*, 91, and 126.

11. *The Cosmic Blueprint*, 203.

12. Thomas Berry, *The Dream of the Earth*, p. 132. See also pp. 16 and 128.

13. Here Rahner's thought is close to that of Teilhard de Chardin, and his concept of the noosphere. See *The Phenomenon of Man*, 200–278, and *Human Energy* (London: Collins, 1969) 113–162.

14. "Christology Within an Evolutionary View . . . ," 172.

15. *Foundations of Christian Faith*, 189.

16. The concept of "companionship" does not come from Rahner. It is developed in an article referred to in the first chapter of this book, by Michael Himes and Kenneth Himes, "The Sacrament of Creation: Towards an Environmental Theology."

17. Jacques Monod, *Chance and Necessity* (London: Collins, 1972) 110. On this whole issue see D.J. Bartholomew, *God and Chance* (London: SCM, 1984). Juan Luis Segundo has integrated the concept of chance into a theological approach to Jesus in his *An Evolutionary Approach to Jesus of Nazareth*. Arthur Peacocke has shown how a creative interplay of chance and law is congruent with theism in his *God and the New Biology*. Rahner does not seem to have allowed that a scientific understanding of the place of chance in evolution could be integrated within purposeful theism. In *Foundations of Christian Faith*, he states that "chance" is not a meaningful term for natural science (pp. 188–189). This is one of the few places where Rahner seems quite out of touch with modern science.

18. Paul Davies, *The Cosmic Blueprint* (London: Unwin Hyman, 1987, 1989).

19. Entropy is the measure of disorder in a system. The second law of thermodynamics states that the entropy, or disorder, of an isolated system always increases.

20. The Nobel prizewinner Ilya Prigogine and the Brussels school have carried out intensive research on the mechanisms of self-organization in dissipative structures in open systems. See G. Nicolis and I.

Prigogine, *Self-Organization in Non-Equilibrium Systems* (New York: Wiley, 1977); Ilya Prigogine and Isabelle Stengers, *Order Out of Chaos* (London: Heinemann, 1984). M. Eigen, and his colleagues at Göttingen, have been researching the development of populations of large self-copying molecules. On the whole issue of self-organization at the heart of the processes of the universe see Erich Jantsch, *The Self-Organizing Universe* (Oxford: Pergammon, 1980); Fritjov Capra, *The Tao of Physics* (Wildwood Press, 1975). For a critical reflection from a theological perspective on the work of Capra, Davies, and Prigogine and Stengers, see Barrie Brundell, "God, Creation and the 'New Physics,'" *Compass* 21 (Summer 1987) 19–22.

21. This is fully argued in Paul Davies' *The Cosmic Blueprint*. Of course Teilhard de Chardin's whole argument is built upon the principle of increasing complexity and its relationship to increasing consciousness. See *The Phenomenon Of Man* (London: Collins, 1959) 66 and 328. See also his *Man's Place in Nature: The Human Zoological Group* (London: Collins, 1966). Juan Luis Segundo is a contemporary theologian who attempts to take seriously both entropy and negentropy, not only in general evolution, but in the history of Jesus of Nazareth, and in Christian life today. See his *An Evolutionary Approach to Jesus of Nazareth*.

22. The story of recent work on "chaos" has been told by James Gleick in his *Chaos: Making a New Science* (London: Penguin Books, 1987).

23. *The Cosmic Blueprint*, 198.

24. J.E. Lovelock, *Gaia: A New Look at Life on Earth* (Oxford University Press, 1979).

25. James Lovelock, *The Ages of Gaia: A Biography of Our Living Earth* (New York: W.W. Norton, 1988) 19.

26. Thomas Aquinas, *Summa Theologiae*, 1.45.1.

27. *Ibid.* 1.45.3.

28. *Ibid.* 1.22.3; 1.23.8.

29. "Natural Science and Reasonable Faith," 31.

30. Christology in the Setting . . . ," 219.

31. A particular question arises from the traditional Catholic understanding, affirmed by Pius XII in *Humani Generis* in 1950, concerning God's special creation of the human soul. Rahner argues that if we see the divine causality as the dynamic ground and bearer of all evolution,

and we understand this divine causality as specified toward the emergence of the human spirit, then "one can say that the divine causality that bears the evolution in general, in the way that it must be operating *here,* can be identified with the 'creation of the soul' in the way in which Pius XII teaches" ("Natural Science and Reasonable Faith," 45). On all of this see Michael Schmaus, *Dogma 2: God and Creation* (London: Sheed and Ward, 1969) 122–144.

32. See Rahner's *Hominisation: The Evolutionary Origin of Man as a Theological Problem* (New York: Herder and Herder, 1965); "Evolution: II Theological," in *Encyclopedia of Theology: A Concise Sacramentum Mundi* (London: Burns and Oates, 1975) 478–488; "Christology within an Evolutionary View . . . ," 165; "Christology in the Setting . . . ," 215–229; *Foundations of Christian Faith,* 185. For the image of "pressure" see "Natural Science and Reasonable Faith," 37.

33. "Christology in the Setting . . . ," 224.

4

The Story of Jesus of Nazareth

Christian theology cannot be satisfied with showing the relationship between evolving creation and the divine power energizing creation from within. It needs to go further and ask: What relationship is there between the story of the universe and the story of Jesus of Nazareth?

To ask this question, however, is to raise the whole issue of what we can really know about the historical Jesus. This chapter will be an attempt to tell the story of Jesus in the light of contemporary biblical scholarship. The specific, concrete, limited, historical figure of Jesus of Nazareth will provide content to all later talk about the cosmic role of the risen Christ.

There are, of course, four stories of Jesus readily available in the gospels of Matthew, Mark, Luke and John. It has long been recognized, however, that these are all stories of believers, and that they express the faith of the believing communities forty to sixty years after the death of Jesus. It is not easy for the modern reader to work out which parts of these stories are historical in the modern sense, and which parts are to be seen as later developments reflecting the faith of the post-Easter church.

Scholars of the eighteenth and nineteenth centuries worked hard to uncover an historically accurate picture of Jesus.[1] Their efforts were significant, although it has become obvious that their picture of Jesus reflected their own convictions and prejudices. Albert Schweitzer, at the turn of the century, offered a comprehensive critique of this whole movement, pointing out how the original search for the historical Jesus had obscured the eschatological and apocalyptic dimensions of the gospels.[2]

In the early part of the twentieth century the focus of scholarship was less on the historical Jesus, and more on studying the development of the tradition concerning Jesus in the early church (form criticism). Biblical scholars were interested in what happened in the period between the life of Jesus and the writing of the gospels. Later, they turned their attention to the theology of the individual gospel writers and their communities (redaction criticism). During the first half of the twentieth century many scholars like the great Rudolf Bultmann, were relatively uninterested in the historical Jesus, and somewhat skeptical about what could be known about him.

Since 1953, however, there has been an extremely important change.[3] Scholars have begun to use the critical tools, honed by Bultmann and others, in a "new quest" for the historical Jesus. Confronted with texts coming from forty to sixty years after the time of Jesus, they work back to the time of Jesus by allowing for three stages in the development of the gospel tradition: the words and deeds of Jesus, the preaching of the early church, and the influence of the gospel writer and the writer's community.[4]

Biblical scholars use a number of criteria in their historical work. Two of these are multiple attestation and dissimilarity. Multiple attestation refers to a situation where something is attributed to Jesus across so many different strands and strata of the New Testament tradition that it can be assumed to be historical. The criterion of dissimilarity comes into play where something attributed to Jesus is so different from the concerns of the later church community, and so dissimilar to the general trends of Judaism, that there is a strong presumption that it is to be attributed to Jesus himself.

Using these and other criteria a body of critically assessed information has been gradually gathered. New discoveries are tested against this consensus in a process of mutual correction. This process has been going on for forty years, and for much longer in the work of scholars like Jeremias and Dodd who stood outside the tradition of Bultmann. There has been critical evaluation of the results across national and denominational lines.

There is international agreement that it is possible to uncover a limited but highly significant amount of information
about the historical Jesus. It is this information which I will attempt to summarize below. Needless to say there would be dis-
agreements about where the emphasis should fall in this kind of
presentation. Any such outline is influenced by the preoccupations of the presenter. My own interpretative standpoint has already been made obvious in this book.

Jesus as Mystic

Jesus was a mystic, someone possessed and led by the Spirit
of God. All the gospels begin the ministry of Jesus with his baptism by the prophetic figure John the Baptist. The accounts of the
descent of the Spirit upon Jesus place him in the charismatic and
prophetic stream of Judaism. This stream includes the great holy
figures of the past like Moses, Elijah, Isaiah and Ezekiel, those
closer to the time of Jesus like Honi the Circle Drawer and Hanina
ben Dosa, and the whole mystical tradition of rabbinic Judaism.

We know that Jesus was not only led by the Spirit, but also
someone radically caught up in a warm, all-embracing relationship with the living God. As a faithful Jew, he would have recited
the Shema twice a day, saying: "You shall love the Lord your God
with all your heart, and with all your soul, and with all your
strength." His own personal experience of God led him to address
God as Abba, a family word like Dad or Papa, expressing intimacy,
boundless trust and great commitment.[5] We know that Jesus
taught his disciples to pray this way, and many years after his
death the Greek-speaking Christian communities still used this
Aramaic word for God, made sacred by the practice of Jesus.[6]

Jesus was a teacher of Wisdom. His use of proverbs and parables placed him within the Wisdom tradition of Israel. Several
times in the gospels we find him speaking of God as Wisdom, and

in the light of the fact that Jesus' style of teaching situated him clearly within the Wisdom tradition, it is likely that these sayings reflect the historical fact: Jesus knew God not only as Abba but also in and through the feminine image of Holy Wisdom.[7]

If God can be addressed familiarly as Abba, then everything else in life is different. This mystical center of Jesus' life is directly connected to his identity and his mission. Schillebeeckx writes that Jesus' Abba experience is "source and secret of his being, message and manner of life."[8] It is the experience of a God who is on our side, a God for human beings, wanting their well-being and happiness. It is "an immediate awareness of God as a power cherishing people and making them free."[9] The foundation for everything else in the life of Jesus is a humanizing and liberating view of God.

Jesus drew on another image to express God's liberating engagement with the world, the ancient Hebrew image of God's rule, the "kingdom of God." This is a symbolic expression capable of many meanings. At the most basic level it is a metaphor for the saving action of God.

For a revolutionary Jew it could mean replacing Roman rule with a Jewish sovereign state. For a Pharisee it could mean allowing God to rule over one's own life through fidelity to the torah. Exactly what it meant for Jesus can best be judged from his liberating deeds and his preaching. These express the significance of the kingdom of God for Jesus. It is through examining the whole ministry of Jesus that we get an accurate picture of what he meant by the symbol "kingdom of God."

What is clear is that the concept of the kingdom of God points to God's future for the world, but it also points to where this future is already with us. The kingdom is God's future, but it is a future anticipated in the healing, liberating ministry of Jesus. Furthermore, it is a future already present in all the good that ordinary women and men do, in every act of genuine love and in every work of peace and justice.

The image of the kingdom of God draws attention to all the ways in which God is already at work in our world, liberating human beings and renewing the whole of creation. It directs us to a transcendent, always greater God, who escapes our comprehension and our plans, yet who breaks in upon the world, overturning our expectations, calling us to conversion of heart, and to the transformation of structures of oppression.

The God of Jesus, the God who can be addressed as Abba, who can be understood as Holy Wisdom, is the God of creation, the God of the universe, the God who makes the sun rise and sends rain upon the just and the unjust (Mt 5:45). Jesus prayed, often at night, in the Galilean hills. His teaching in parables shows him to be a person who could see the whole of life, nature and human activities as transparent to the divine.

The God who could be addressed as Abba, the God who numbers every hair on our heads, is the God who feeds the birds of the air, and clothes the lilies of the field more gloriously than King Solomon ever clothed himself. Jesus saw the universe as gracious. The God of creation could be trusted radically. At the most fundamental level, he taught his disciples, there is no need for anxiety (Mt 6:25–33).

The Prophetic Impact of Jesus
upon Culture and Society

The social and cultural world of Palestine was in crisis during the lifetime of Jesus although Galilee experienced some political stability during the rule of Herod Antipas. The practice of the torah, which gave meaning and direction to Jewish life, was made difficult by the Roman occupation, with its competing and alien political and legal system, and its exploitative taxation. There were large numbers of displaced and unemployed people, some of them forced off their land by the combination of Jewish tithing responsibilities and Roman taxation. Representatives of Rome were often insensitive to Jewish religious feelings, and sometimes extraordinarily brutal. Those who "farmed" taxes for Rome, and the workers who collected the taxes, were hated and despised.

Every society has its "conventional wisdom," made up of everyday assumptions about life which hold society together and which are usually unquestioned. In first century Palestine, "conventional wisdom" said that fidelity to the torah would lead to God's blessing.[10] This assumption tended to have the side-effect of suggesting that those who faced destitution or some other disaster were being punished by God. Of course many thinkers, like the author of the book of Job, had challenged this thinking, but it remained a "common-sense" understanding for many people, as it does in many Christian circles today.

Conventional wisdom gave a sense of identity in a chaotic situation by creating boundaries, distinguishing Jew from Gentile, male from female, priests, Levites and full Israelites from others, those who were well from those possessed by evil, the wealthy from the poor, the respectable from the outcast, the righteous from the public sinner.

In response to the Roman occupation it seemed important to close ranks and resist assimilation. A high value was placed upon keeping oneself separate from all that was unclean. In first century Palestine it seemed the way of survival as well as the way of fidelity. Each of the major renewal groups in Palestine, the Essenes, the Pharisees and the revolutionary movement, intensified, in its own way, the ideal of separation from all that was unclean. The main sanction against those who did not conform to the code of separation from all that was unclean was to ostracize the offenders, and deny them table fellowship. This, too, has been the case in Christian communities.

In this context, Jesus set out on his mission of renewal in fidelity to the God who was Abba. He preached and acted as if the new age of God's rule was imminent, indeed already breaking in, and he called his hearers to conversion of mind and heart. His view of God brought him into direct conflict with the conventional wisdom and the ideal of separation from what was unclean. Jesus systematically challenged the social pattern of exclusivity and sought to replace it with one based upon compassion.

He did this by way of two options: first, he gave priority to men and women in his interpretation of the torah: second, he gave priority to the poor, the hurt and the outcast.

Jesus, like some other Jewish thinkers, saw the whole torah as centered on the two great commandments of love of God and love of neighbor, from Deuteronomy 6:4–5 and Leviticus 19:18. For him it was clear that the deepest meaning of the torah was compassion. It expressed God's compassion for men and women. This is why Jesus could say that "the sabbath was made for the human being, not the human being for the sabbath" (Mk 2:27). The sabbath was about "doing good" and "saving life" (Mk 3:4). In other words, the sabbath was about compassion.

For the same reason Jesus rejected the demands of ritual purity—"there is nothing outside a human being which by going in can defile a person, but the things which come out are what defiles a human being" (Mk 7:16). Jesus internalized the torah and radicalized it on his own authority: "You have heard it said . . . now I say to you . . ." (Mt 5:17–48).[11]

At the heart of all this is the issue of who God is. Jesus' proclamation of this "humanizing" criterion for the interpretation of the torah is the direct overflow of the experience of God as Abba. It is to be understood as part of the preaching and practice of the reign of God.[12] God's reign has the well-being of human beings, and the world, as its focus.

What contemporary theology calls the "option for the poor" finds expression both in the practice of Jesus and in his preaching. The gospels are unambiguous in their record of the priority Jesus gave to three groups in Israel: first, the economically poor and oppressed; second, those who were diseased, disabled or possessed;

third, those who were outcasts because they were prostitutes, tax collectors or in some other way public sinners.

This option found very specific expression in Jesus' meals with outcasts and sinners (Mk 2:15). In these meals, those who were untouchable experienced themselves accepted as friends. Jesus did not shrink from their touch (Lk 7:38), but welcomed them into meals which were really anticipatory celebrations of the coming kingdom of God. These meals were a pledge of God's forgiveness and an invitation to conversion.

They provoked hostile reactions, and Luke records one of them: "Behold, a glutton and a drunkard, a friend of tax collectors and sinners" (7:34). The truth is that Jesus not only proclaimed good news, he himself was good news. Schillebeeckx has captured this idea with his saying that Jesus' dealings with people liberated them and made them glad. He writes that being sad in the presence of the historical Jesus was "an existential impossibility."[13]

The priority for the outcast also found expression in sharp confrontations with those in power. Jesus severely criticized those who laid heavy burdens on the poor and defenseless.[14] He could say to them: "Truly, I say to you, the tax collectors and the harlots go into the kingdom of God before you" (Mt 21:31).

Jesus was universal in his outreach and love. No group and no person was excluded. But this inclusive love was truly universal precisely because of the option for the poor, the sick and the outcast. Only through such an option could Jesus love both the poorest, by standing with them and offering them the good news of the kingdom, and the dominant groups, by challenging them from the side of the poor and inviting them to conversion.

The option for the outcast is expressed in parables, above all in the great parables of the lost sheep, the lost coin and the prodigal son, all of which describe God's joy ("there is more joy in heaven . . . ") in finding the lost; it is powerfully expressed in the parable of the laborers in the vineyard, which forces us to consider a God of sheer grace. Jesus' defense of his option for outcasts is to say that this is the way God is. The option for the poor expresses a truth about God.

In fidelity to his experience of God as Abba, Jesus deliberately subverted the social and religious structures of separation both through his humanizing approach to the torah and his choice to be with, and stand with, the poor, the sick, the public sinners and all who were outcasts.

The New Community

Jesus' prophetic commitment was not directed simply to people as individuals, nor was it a general appeal to the world at large. Rather, he set out to form a movement of renewal. He called his hearers into a distinct social group which had as its aim the gathering of Israel, and the religious renewal of Israel.[15] It would be in and through the renewal of all Israel that the whole world would come to share in the salvation offered by God.

Jesus called men and women to discipleship, a discipleship which was unusual in that it was Jesus who did the calling, and the disciples were called into a lifelong relationship with him. They never "graduated" but remained permanently disciples. Their focus was on Jesus and his liberating message of the kingdom of God, rather than on the interpretation of the torah.

We can distinguish two groups among the followers of Jesus: first there were those, like Joseph of Arimathea (Mk 15:42–47), Zacchaeus (Lk 19:1–10), Mary and Martha and Lazarus (Jn 11:1), who accepted the message of Jesus, but remained in their own place living as faithful members of the new community; then there were those, like Simon, Andrew, James and John (Mk 1:16–20), and Mary of Magdala, Mary the mother of James and Salome (Mk 15:40–41), who left everything and followed after him.

The group of disciples constituted a new family, a new household. Jesus promised them that here and now, within his community, they would discover a new group of mothers, sisters and brothers (Mk 3:31–35; 10:29–31; Lk 11:27–28). Fathers are not mentioned, and the disciples are instructed: "Call no one on earth your father" (Mt 23:8–12). With a God who was Abba, there was apparently no place in the new community for the role of the patriarchal father.[16]

This does not mean that there were no structures within the community of disciples. There is evidence that Jesus gave Peter a unique leadership role in the new community.[17] It is also clear that Jesus set up a group of twelve, who were called to missionary work, and whose institution as a group was a prophetic, symbolic act, pointing to the restoration of the twelve tribes of Israel (Mt 19:28).[18]

The new community was a place of equality and inclusivity. Elisabeth Schüssler Fiorenza has described it as a "discipleship of equals." In this movement "tax collectors, sinners, women, children, fishers, housewives, those who had been healed of their infirmities or set free from bondage from evil spirits" all found their place, confident in their dignity and equality as God's beloved children.[19] Children and slaves were brought to the center of the new community and became the model of discipleship (Mk 10:15; 9:35–37; 10:43; Mt 18:1–4; Lk 9:48; 22:27). The community was called to a "solidarity from below with the victims of a feudal society."[20]

Women and men shared in discipleship, and the women who followed Jesus played a central role at the cross and in the resurrection experiences of the early church. In Galatians, Paul expresses the early church's conviction about the meaning of baptism in a community of equals: "For as many of you as were baptized into Christ have put on Christ. There is neither Jew nor Greek, there is neither slave nor free, there is neither male nor female; for you are all one in Christ Jesus" (3:28).

Jesus did not oppose positive use of power. On the contrary he embodied it in himself, and encouraged it in others. But he explicitly and consistently prohibited every form of dominating power within the new community (Mk 10:42–45). Domination was to be replaced by *diakonia,* authority exercised like a servant. There was to be no oppression, no coercion, no violence directed to anyone inside or outside the community. New Testament scholar Gerhard Lohfink has written:

> On the basis of Jesus' conduct, Mark 10:42–45 defines with disturbing consistency every possible form of authority within the church. Nonviolence, renunciation of domination and consequent vulnerability are irrevocably embedded in the church and its offices by the practice of Jesus.[21]

This kind of *diakonia* is not passivity, but the attempt to win over one's opponents by persuasion, witness to the truth, and moving toward them with love. Authority as *diakonia* is a vulnerable authority. It was a relational and collaborative use of power which Jesus consistently opposed to domination and violence.[22]

Jesus' Powerful Acts of Liberation and Healing

The ancient world took the miraculous as part of life. Signs and wonders were, however, understood differently from one culture to another around the Mediterranean. In the Greco-Roman world the cults of Asklepios and Isis were directed toward the health and well-being of individuals. On the other hand, apocalyptic communities tended to see miracles and wonders as signs of the coming divine victory. The historian Josephus saw them as portents revealing the divine purpose in history.[23]

Charismatic religious leaders, like Jesus' younger contemporary Hanina ben Dosa, were healers. It is reported that Hanina ben Dosa healed Rabbi Gamaliel from a distance.[24] The New Testament takes it for granted that not only Jesus, but his disciples, and others not connected with him, could drive out evil spirits and heal the sick.[25]

Some of the stories of Jesus doing marvelous deeds may be projections back into the life of Jesus of post-Easter experience. There is a tendency for the tradition concerning marvelous actions to grow. We can find this tendency at work even between Mark's and Matthew's accounts of the same stories: many sick (Mk 1:34) becomes all the sick (Mt 8:16); one blind man (Mk 10:46) becomes two (Mt 20:30); one possessed (Mk 5:2) becomes two (Mt 8:28). If we find this tendency for the tradition concerning marvels to develop between the writings of Mark and Matthew, then we have to presume that the same process was at work in the period before the gospels were written.

However the healing activity of Jesus is deeply embedded in the gospel tradition. It is attested to so widely that it must be considered to be based in history. The sabbath healings, and the controversy they provoked, and the exorcisms, which led to the charge that Jesus was in league with Beelzebul, belong to the earliest tradition about Jesus. There is no doubt that Jesus was a charismatic healer and exorcist. His great acts of healing left a deep impact on the movement he left behind.

Jesus usually drove out demons simply by a verbal command. The response to this among the people was amazement at the authority Jesus possessed (Mk 1:27). His opponents did not deny this power, but questioned its source.[26] When Jesus healed it was often by touch. According to the gospels, the healings were even more frequent than the exorcisms. As well as the summary accounts describing large numbers of healings, there are thirteen stories in the synoptic gospels which describe healings from specific maladies: fever (Mk 1:29–31), leprosy (Mk 1:40–45; Lk 17:11–19), paralysis (Mk 2:1–12), withered hand (Mk 3:1–6), bent back (Lk 13:10–17), hemorrhage (Mk 5:24b–34), deafness and speech impediment (Mk 7:37), blindness (Mk 8:22–26; 10:46–

52), dropsy (Lk 14:1-6), severed ear (Lk 22:51), and a sickness near death or paralysis (Lk 7:1-10; Mt 8:5-13).[27]

According to the gospels themselves, miracles are ambiguous: they can lead to faith, but they are open to other interpretations, such as that Jesus cured by the power of evil (Mk 3:22-30). Jesus rejected as temptation the idea of spectacular and authenticating miracles.[28] He saw his own acts of healing as expressions of God's compassion for the hurt of the world, and as anticipations of God's coming kingdom (Lk 7:22; 11:20). They express God's desire to liberate men and women from suffering, and they function as a sign and a promise of God's future salvation.

The healing ministry shows that this salvation is far more than a religious matter in the narrow sense of the word "religious." It is a physical, bodily matter. It embraces health, sanity, relationships, community, and wholeness. God's salvation is revealed as something embracing the whole of reality.

Schillebeeckx suggests that Jesus saw a vision of final salvation in and through his own fragmentary actions of doing good. These were, necessarily, historical and finite. This has important implications for those who follow Jesus: the limited healing ministry of Jesus "confirms the permanent validity of any practice of doing good which is incomplete because it is historically limited."[29]

Preacher of the Reign of God

Jesus taught in proverb and parable and he did this with extraordinary skill. He was a teacher of Wisdom, standing within the ancient Wisdom tradition. Yet there was something unique and radical about Jesus' use of traditional Wisdom forms. His own proverbs and parables are distinctive, and by and large they are considered to be authentic creations of the historical Jesus.[30]

Traditional proverbs contained a flash of insight, which often directed the hearer to live faithfully and well before God and the community. They tended to tell the hearer how to live a proper and orderly life. Jesus' proverbial sayings were extremely intense, often using hyperbole to jolt the hearer into a radically new perception of life.[31] They were not so much aimed at orderly existence as at raising fundamental questions and challenging settled patterns. They seemed aimed at creating the space necessary if the hearers were to be open to the mystery of life and of God. They were meant to mediate an experience of the kingdom.

The following are typical proverbial sayings of Jesus: "But many that are first will be last and the last first" (Mk 10:31); "Leave the dead to bury their own dead" (Lk 9:60); "It is easier for a camel to go through the eye of a needle than for a rich man to enter the kingdom of God" (Mk 10:25); "If anyone strikes you on the right cheek, turn to him the other also" (Mt 5:39); "Love your enemies and pray for those who persecute you" (Mt 5:44). In the shock, confusion and challenge that these sayings would have provoked, Jesus' hearers were invited into a bigger world, the world of the kingdom. To hold together in one's heart and mind "love" and the "enemy," the person or group one has been taught to hate, is to experience the kingdom already breaking in upon one's life.

The parables function in a similar way. They are usually realistic stories or pictures which get the hearer interested. At the heart of the story there is often an "unexpected turn," a dramatic reversal to what the hearer expects, which opens up a new world.[32] The story functions like a poetic metaphor: it contains a shock to the imagination, which conveys a new vision.[33] The parable of the workers in the vineyard, for example, would have seemed very ordinary and easily understood, until the moment when the owner pays everybody the same amount. The apparent injustice here creates the unexpected turn, the shock to the imagination. It invites the hearer to a new vision of God, of the poor and outcast, and of oneself before a bountiful and gracious God. It mediates an experience of God. To hear such a parable with "ears to hear" is to experience the presence of the kingdom already present.

In the famous parable of the good Samaritan, the imaginative shock is often missed today. For Jesus' hearers it would have occurred when the priest and levite have gone past the injured traveler and the one who represents all that is hated stops and gives help. The hearers are invited to imagine themselves abandoned and dying, passed by their own leaders, then saved by the boundless generosity of the specific enemy they despised and hated. To hold together the idea of one's own real enemy and the possibility that such a person is warm and extremely generous— this is to know something of the reign of God.

The parables of Jesus are works of art, the products of someone who thought spontaneously in images. The images come from the whole of life: the beauty of wild flowers, the growth of trees from tiny seeds, crops of grain, bread rising, a woman sweeping a floor looking for what was lost, children playing games, the relationship between a shepherd and the sheep, the generosity of a parent to a wayward son. The parables reflect an observation and a love for both nature and human affairs. They reveal that Jesus saw God at the heart of nature and at the heart of human society.

C.H. Dodd said long ago that the realism of the parables of Jesus "arises from a conviction that here is no mere analogy, but an inward affinity, between the natural order and the spiritual order."[34] According to this great biblical scholar, "the sense of the divineness of the natural order is the major premise of all the parables."[35]

Jesus was not simply communicating in parable about the kingdom. Rather, hearers who were open to the parable were being led to experience the kingdom in and through the parable. The parables mediate the experience of the kingdom. Furthermore, there is an intrinsic link between the religious experience of Jesus and the parables in which that experience is expressed.[36] Jesus, an artist in his use of parable, mediated what he experienced through his art. We are very close indeed to Jesus of Nazareth when we listen with open ears to the parables of the kingdom.

The Death of Jesus and the Experience of Resurrection

The execution of Jesus was a consequence of his preaching and behavior. He preached and acted in fidelity to God, with all the radical consequences this had for social and religious institutions, and this led to confrontation with those in power. He preached a God of the outcast and sinner, and this led to his own death outside the city, as one of the godless. Schillebeeckx has written: "The death of Jesus was no coincidence, but the intrinsic historical outcome of the radicalism of both his message and lifestyle, which showed that all 'master-servant' relationships were incompatible with the kingdom of God."[37]

His death came as a result of a life lived in fidelity to the demands of love. The cross was the final expression of the unconditional character of Jesus' commitment. He so identified himself with God, and this God's concern for humanity, that he accepted the consequences, the experience of profound failure, desertion by most of his community, and even seeming abandonment by the God in whom he had trusted. Suffering and death "for others" expressed the unconditional nature of Jesus' life lived "for others."[38]

Jesus was executed by the Romans as a troublemaker and a political rebel, in spite of his rejection of the revolutionaries' program. This shameful death should have meant the end of him as a force to be reckoned with. But history shows otherwise. It reveals that the disciples of Jesus had powerful experiences after the death of Jesus, experiences which they expressed as encounters with Jesus, risen and triumphant over death.

The importance of these Easter experiences cannot be exaggerated. Easter faith was a totally unlikely response to the devastation of the cross. The experiences of the risen Jesus were many and varied. Paul described them in what was already a traditional formula, in a relatively early part of the New Testament period, and at a time when many of the witnesses were still alive (1 Cor 15). The energy and confidence, and the very existence, of the believing community can only be explained on the basis of these new experiences on the part of the disciples.

These experiences were understood as God's vindication of Jesus, in his claim to speak for God, in his identification with the poor, in his assurance of salvation. They were experienced as God's salvation triumphing over sin, death and all need to prove oneself righteous. Salvation, justification, redemption, liberation—these were just some of the images used to describe God's action "for us" in the life, death and resurrection of Jesus of Nazareth.

These experiences were understood as an encounter with Jesus as the exalted and risen Lord, the Christ, the Son of God. Sebastian Moore has argued that the first resurrection experiences were already an experience of what would be articulated later as the divinity of Jesus Christ.[39] He argues that, during the ministry of Jesus, the God whom the disciples had found through Jesus would have been so real and vivid as to make old religious traditions seem pale and empty by comparison. With the whole of their religious faith caught up in the ecstatic experience of following Jesus, the disciples would have experienced his failure and death as the death of their faith, the death of God.

There was a "psychological displacement" of faith in God for the disciples in the death of Jesus. Divinity was rediscovered in the encounter with the risen Christ. The risen Jesus was experienced as God's presence. In these meetings there is already the experiential ground for the affirmations of faith in Jesus which would emerge in the New Testament period, and in later church doctrine.

The divine sonship of Jesus was read back into the life of Jesus from the experience of resurrection. In the light of the Jewish Wisdom tradition, Jesus was identified with the Wisdom of God and the Word of God, and understood as having a cosmic role. The hymn of the opening chapter of Colossians (verses 15–20) plainly understands all of creation as closely related to Jesus Christ: first, from the beginning, all of creation is directed toward Christ ("in him all things were created"); second, as the first-born from the dead, the risen Christ has a role of cosmic reconciliation ("through him to reconcile to himself all things, whether on earth or in heaven").

These themes appear in John's gospel, with its unambiguous theology of the pre-existence of the Word, and the concept that all things were made through the Word (1:1–14), and in Ephesians, with its theology of the recapitulation of all of creation in the risen Christ (1:10).

This doctrine of recapitulation of all things in Christ would become central to the synthesis of Irenaeus of Lyons, perhaps the first great systematic theologian. He opposed the dualism of the Gnostics with a theology which unified creation and redemption. The cosmic role of the Word of God, the Logos, continued to be a key idea in the theology of the fourth and fifth centuries, where the Word was understood not only as the beginning but as the goal (the *telos*) of the cosmos.[40]

In 451, at the Council of Chalcedon, the Christian church declared its faith in Jesus Christ, consubstantial with the Father as to Godhead, consubstantial with us as to humanity, one Christ, made known in two natures; these two natures, it was declared, exist "without confusion, without change, without division, without separation"; and, the council taught, these two natures are united in one person (one *prosopon* and one *hypostasis*).[41] With these expressions the council affirmed and sought to protect the Christian community's most fundamental convictions about the identity of Jesus of Nazareth.

NOTES

1. The "quest" for the historical Jesus began in 1778 with the posthumous publication of an essay by Hermann Samuel Reimarus (1694–1768) One of the significant nineteenth century contributions was the two volume work by David Friedrich Strauss, *Life of Jesus* (1835).

2. Albert Schweitzer, *The Quest of the Historical Jesus* (New York: Macmillan, 1959), first published in German in 1906.

3. In 1953 Ernst Kasemann formally began a new quest for the historical Jesus from within the school of Bultmann with an address entitled "The Problem of the Historical Jesus." For a discussion of this "new quest" see James M. Robinson, *A New Quest for the Historical Jesus and Other Essays* (Philadelphia: Fortress Press, 1983).

4. This approach was endorsed officially for the Catholic Church in *The Instruction on the Historical Truth of the Gospels,* by the Pontifical Biblical Commission (1964). It can be found, with a commentary, in Joseph A. Fitzmyer, *A Christological Catechism: New Testament Answers* (New York: Paulist Press, 1982) 131–140.

5. Mk 14:36. On Jesus' spirituality see Joachim Jeremias, *The Prayers of Jesus* (London: SCM, 1967); Edward Schillebeeckx, *Jesus: An Experiment in Christology* (New York: Seabury Press, 1979); James A. Dunn, *Jesus and the Spirit* (London: SCM, 1975); Elisabeth Schüssler Fiorenza, *In Memory of Her: A Feminist Theological Reconstruction of Christian Origins* (London: SCM, 1983) 130–140; Donald Goergen, *The Mission and Ministry of Jesus* (Wilmington: Michael Glazier, 1986) 129–145. Dunn develops the idea that Jesus related to God as Spirit, as well as Abba, while Schüssler Fiorenza develops the idea of Jesus' relationship with God as *Sophia.*

6. Gal 4:6; Rom 8:15.

7. Lk 7:35; 11:49; cf. Mt 11:28–30; Lk 13:34.

8. Schillebeeckx, *Jesus*, 256–271.

9. *Ibid*. 268.

10. I have been influenced in the idea of Jesus as challenge to conventional wisdom by the insights of Marcus J. Borg. See his *Jesus, A New Vision: Spirit, Culture and the Life of Discipleship* (San Francisco: Harper and Row, 1987). I prefer to avoid Borg's expression "politics of holiness" because "holiness" means far more than separation from what is unclean, and it has been, and still is, an important theological concept for Judaism, and for Christianity.

11. Schillebeeckx notes that Jesus' teaching means "that the praxis of the kingdom of God cannot really be 'laid down' in juridical laws (however much the actual business of living may sometimes call for them). It may demand at times that one do more than what the Law lays down; it may however also require one to go against what the Law specifies. At the same time that poses the lofty requirement that we should seek out God's *kairos* or propitious moment in the concrete circumstances of life" (*Jesus*, 242).

12. The expression "humanizing criterion" comes from Schillebeeckx. See his *On Christian Faith: The Spiritual, Ethical, and Political Dimensions* (New York: Crossroad., 1987) 28.

13. E. Schillebeeckx, *Jesus*, 200–229.

14. It is important to remember, however, that the controversies described in the gospels between Jesus and the scribes and Pharisees (Mk 7:1–23; Lk 11:37–54; Mt 23) reflect the later antagonism between Judaism and the Christian community which was emerging from within Judaism. Jesus was a Jew and the original controversies were part of inner-Jewish dialogue.

15. On this new community see Gerhard Lohfink, *Jesus and Community: The Social Dimension of Christian Faith* (New York: Paulist Press, 1964); Elisabeth Schüssler Fiorenza, *In Memory of Her;* Frederick J. Cwiekowski, *The Beginning of the Church* (New York: Paulist Press, 1988); Raymond Brown, *The Churches the Apostles Left Behind* (New York: Paulist Press, 1984); Edward Schillebeeckx, *The Church with a Human Face: A New and Expanded Theology of Ministry* (New York: Crossroad, 1985).

62 JESUS AND THE COSMOS

16. See G. Lohfink, *Jesus and Community*, 44–50; E. Schüssler Fiorenza, *In Memory of Her*, 140–151.

17. Gal 1:18–2:14; 1 Cor 9:5; 1 Cor 15:5; Mt 16:18; Jn 21:15–17. On this see Raymond Brown, Karl Donfried, and John Reumann (editors), *Peter in the New Testament* (New York: Paulist Press, 1973).

18. The earliest evidence for a special group of twelve is 1 Cor 15:5. The list of names vary, indicating that it was the symbol of the twelve that mattered (Mt 10:2; Mk 3:16–19; Lk 6:14–16; Acts 1:13). In discussions of the maleness of the twelve it is important to remember that the twelve tribes took their names from the twelve sons of Jacob.

19. Schüssler Fiorenza, *In Memory of Her*, 135.

20. *Ibid.* 148.

21. Gerhard Lohfink, *Jesus and Community*, 117.

22. I have developed these thoughts at more length in *Called To Be Church in Australia: An Approach to the Renewal of Local Churches* (Homebush, N.S.W.: St. Paul Publications, 1987) 93–108.

23. See H.C. Kee, *Miracle and the Early Christian World: A Study in Socio-Historical Method* (New Haven: Yale University Press, 1983). On the miracles in general see R.H. Fuller, *Interpreting the Miracles* (Philadelphia: Westminster, 1963); G. Theissen, *The Miracle Stories of the Early Christian Tradition* (Philadelphia: Fortress Press, 1983).

24. Geza Vermes, *Jesus and the World of Judaism* (London: SCM, 1983) 8.

25. These include the disciples (Mk 6:7–13; 9:18; Mt 10:1–8; Lk 10:17), an unknown stranger using Jesus' name (Mk 9:38), and Pharisaic exorcists (Mt 12:27).

26. See Mk 3:22. In the *Babylonian Talmud* (Sanhedrin 43a) it is said that Jesus was executed because he practiced sorcery and led Israel astray.

27. I have followed Marcus J. Borg in this list. See his *Jesus: A New Vision*, 65 and 73.

28. Lk 4:12; Mk 8:11–13; Lk 11:16, 29.

29. E. Schillebeeckx, *Christ*, 791.

30. On all of this see J. Jeremias, *The Parables of Jesus* (New York: Scribners, 1963); J.D. Crossan, *In Parables* (New York: Harper and Row, 1973); *Cliffs of Fall: Paradox and Polyvalence in the Parables of Jesus* (New York: Seabury, 1980); N. Perrin, *Jesus and the Language of the*

Kingdom (Philadelphia: Fortress, 1976); D.O. Via, *The Parables* (Philadelphia: Fortress, 1966); A. Wilder, *Early Christian Rhetoric* (Cambridge: Harvard University Press, 1971); *Jesus' Parables and the War of Myths* (Philadelphia: Fortress Press, 1982); J. Breech, *The Silence of Jesus* (Philadelphia: Fortress Press, 1983).

31. See W.A. Beardslee, "Uses of the Proverb in the Synoptic Gospels," *Interpretation* 24 (1970) 61–76; N. Perrin, *Jesus and the Language of the Kingdom,* 51.

32. See R.W. Funk, *Language, Hermeneutic and the Word of God* (New York: Harper and Row, 1966) 139.

33. A. Wilder, *Early Christian Rhetoric,* 72.

34. C.H. Dodd, *The Parables of the Kingdom* (Glasgow: Collins, 1961—first published 1935), 20.

35. *Ibid.* 21.

36. On this see J.D. Crossan, *In Parables,* 22.

37. E. Schillebeeckx, *Christ: The Christian Experience in the Modern World* (London: SCM, 1980) 794.

38. *Ibid.* 795.

39. Sebastian Moore, *The Fire and the Rose Are One* (London: Darton, Longman and Todd, 1980).

40. See Jaroslav Pelikan, *Jesus Through the Centuries* (New Haven: Yale University Press, 1985), 57–70.

41. It is important to note that neither *prosopon* nor *hypostasis* was defined at the time, and neither word meant exactly what we mean when we use the word "person" today.

5

The Relationship Between Jesus and the Evolving Cosmos

For God so loved the cosmos that he gave his only Son, that whoever believes in him should not perish but have eternal life. For God sent the Son into the cosmos, not to condemn the cosmos, but that the cosmos might be saved through him (Jn 3:16–17).

In the last chapter I attempted a summary of what we can know about the historical Jesus on the basis of recent scholarship. While this does not amount to anything like a modern biography, it does bring us up against a real person with specific characteristics and preoccupations. It enables us to glimpse something of the attractive power of this person, and to understand his historical impact. It enables Christians to grasp in more detail the preaching and practice of the one they follow.

Christians believe that this specific person, who endorsed some views and not others, who chose to make some options and reject others, is the revelation of God in and to the world. Because Jesus of Nazareth is understood as the Word made flesh, the "filling out" of our picture of Jesus is also a "filling out" of what is revealed in him.

It is not that faith depends upon historical research. A person who has no access to historical studies concerning Jesus can have great faith in him. But historical research can clarify and amplify the content of faith in Jesus. It makes a difference that Jesus really did address God as Abba. It is highly significant to believers of the late twentieth century that the historical Jesus made a specific option for the poor, the sick and the outcast.

What relationship is there between this particular, individual figure, Jesus of Nazareth, and the evolving universe of late twentieth century science? What relationship is there between the story of Jesus and the story of the cosmos?

The following principles from Rahner's theology can be brought into play to illuminate the relationship between these two stories: first, Jesus can be understood as the self-transcendence of the cosmos toward God; second, there is an intrinsic inter-relationship between God's communication in grace to all people and God's action in Jesus of Nazareth; third, Jesus can be understood, from God's side, as God's self-communication to the cosmos. In a later section of this book I will need to focus particularly on the relationship between the risen Christ and the material universe.

Jesus of Nazareth—Self-Transcendence of the Cosmos into God

In 1957 four scientists (Burbridge, Burbridge, Fowler and Hoyle) published a classic paper in the scientific journal *Reviews of Modern Physics* which showed how all the naturally occurring elements (except hydrogen and helium) are built up inside the stars, through a process called nucleosynthesis. John Gribbin writes of his own reaction on reading this paper: "I still recall the thrill I got when I first came across the paper as a graduate student in 1966; the awe of knowing that the equations in the paper I held explained where all the atoms in my own body (except for the primordial hydrogen) came from, and how all those atoms had been cooked in stars."[1]

Our Sun contains recycled material that comes from older stars, and the Earth is made from this same source. The material of which we humans are made has the same origin. Sixty-five percent of our body weight is oxygen, eighteen percent is carbon, and all of it comes from the process of nucleosynthesis inside stars. David Ellyard comments on this process:

In this way was made all the iron we now find in our blood, all the phosphorus and calcium that strengthens our bones, all the sodium and potassium that drives signals along our nerves. Atoms so formed are thrown off into space by aged stars in their death throes. Natural forces recycle them into new stars, into planets and plants and people. We are all made of stardust.[2]

In this context, the ancient truth taught in the Council of Chalcedon, that Jesus is consubstantial with us in his humanity, possessing a truly human nature, and a human body and soul, can now be restated by saying that Jesus too is made up of elements forged inside the fiery centers of stars. He too is made of stardust.

Jesus is part of this process, a product of the Big Bang, the formation of the Milky Way, the unfolding of our Solar System, the molding of the crust of the Earth, the development of life on the planet, and the emergence of consciousness. He, like us, is the universe come to consciousness, a person truly of the Earth, truly a part of biological evolution.[3]

Jesus is part of the climax of that long development whereby the world becomes aware of itself, and comes into the direct presence of God. He is someone who, like all of us in his finite and historically conditioned humanity, is a receiver of God's self-communication by grace.

Jesus is unlike anyone else, however, in that in him we find a radical and complete openness to God's self-giving in grace. In this one product of evolutionary history, the cosmos accepts God in a definitive and absolute way.

The whole process of the world's self-transcendence into God reaches its climax in the "yes" to God embodied in Jesus' person and life. This "yes" finds expression in Jesus' prayer, in his preaching of a liberating and gracious God, in his acts of healing and liberation, in his critique of oppressive structures, in his partiality for the poor, the sick and the outcast, in his mediation of reconciliation, in his joyous meals, in his confrontation with those who kept others bound, in his relationships, in his formation of a new community and, above all, in his struggle with, and acceptance of, his death as the consequence and outcome of his life.

In all that can be described as Jesus' "obedience," which reaches its climax in the cross, there is spoken the "yes" to God's self-communication that the whole cosmos has been moving toward throughout its history.

Yet the universe could not reach this goal of itself. It occurs through God's grace. When a line continually approaches a curve without meeting it in a finite distance, it is called an asymptote. Rahner makes use of this image to describe creation moving toward the incarnation: the incarnation is "the asymptotic goal of a development of the world reaching out to God."[4]

In the world as we actually find it, a graced world, the history of the cosmos is a history of self-transcendence into the life of God. This reaches its climax in the life, death and resurrection of Jesus of Nazareth. The incarnation is understood as the beginning of the divinization of the world as a whole.

Rahner notes that Gnostic forms of Christianity have always tended to see God approaching humanity purely at the level of the spirit. But the Christian message is that the Word became *flesh,* the Word became *matter.* The word "incarnation" means, literally, "becoming flesh." Rahner states that according to the true teaching of Christianity, "God lays hold of matter when the Logos becomes flesh."[5] Not only can we say that "God lays hold of matter," but we can say that Jesus is the product of the evolutionary history of matter. He is the self-transcendence of the world of matter reaching out to God. And, Rahner claims, this self-transcendence of the cosmos, in its highest and final stage, is identical with the absolute self-communication of God.

The Relationship Between Jesus of Nazareth and God's Universal Self-Communication by Grace

If the whole history of the universe reaches its climax in Jesus of Nazareth, then this raises the question about the connection between Jesus, as self-transcendence of the universe, and the rest of us human beings. Are not we, too, the self-transcendence of the universe? How is what happens in him related to what happens in all of us through God's grace?

We have to say that a real and ultimate self-transcendence of the spirit into God takes place not only in Jesus of Nazareth, but also in all spiritual beings.[6] Grace is offered to every woman and man. Union with God by grace is the destiny of all people, supposing only that they do not choose to reject it.

God's self-communication to creatures, in grace, is the highest stage in the evolutionary process. Evolutionary history reaches its goal in God's communication in love with conscious and free human beings, and, through them, with the whole of creation. As I have already pointed out, in Rahner's theology grace is simply God, always present in self-offering to every human person. This is Rahner's way of describing the core of the good news of the kingdom preached by Jesus, the idea of a gracious, liberating God at the heart of reality.

God is present as offer and call even prior to any human response. The human person is, of course, free to accept or reject this offer. Every human person lives in the presence of this grace. We inhabit a world of grace. Grace is our constant environment. It is the milieu for human existence at every stage of human history. God has chosen, in absolute freedom and transcendence, to be present to everyone as an intrinsic, constitutive principle of human existence.[7]

If it can be said, then, that God's self-communication to the world by grace is the highest stage in the evolutionary process, how are we to understand what happens in Jesus Christ? Are we to understand God's self-communication in Jesus of Nazareth as on an absolutely new and radically higher level compared to the grace that is offered to every human being? Or should we see the incarnation as something that is certainly unique, but which is an inner moment in the universal bestowal of grace?

Rahner argues for the second of these options. He sees the incarnation as an intrinsic and necessary part of God's bestowal of grace upon the whole world. It is only in Jesus that God's self-communication to all creatures reaches its concrete and tangible expression in history. Here at one point in space and time, in one flesh and blood person, God's self-communication is both given irrevocably and accepted radically. In this specific person we find God's promise to all humanity reaching its fulfillment. Here this promise receives visible and tangible expression, and becomes irreversibly part of human history.

There is a further connection between grace in all of us and incarnation in Jesus: the effect of the incarnation on the humanity of Jesus occurs through the same grace given to us. It happens through the very same reality that is offered to us all, God's self-communication in grace. God's giving of God's self to all of us, and the incarnation in Jesus Christ, can only be understood together, and they both occur through the same reality, grace.

What, then, is unique in what happens in Jesus of Nazareth? What is unsurpassable and definitive about this union? It is the fact that here God's self-offering (grace) and human acceptance of this offer occur in such an absolute way that we can say that this is not only something God accomplishes, but it *is* God. While we remain receivers of God's offer, we can say that Jesus *is* God's offer. Jesus not only communicates God's pledge to us, Jesus *is* the pledge of God to us.

In Jesus "a human reality belongs absolutely to God."[8] Here we find an irrevocable unity between the one who offers and what is offered, between the proclaimer and what is proclaimed. In Jesus there is such a union between a human reality and God that we can say that this human proclamation and offer is a reality of God. Here human being and divine self-giving are united in a way that is unmixed, but inseparable, and therefore irrevocable.

So grace for us and incarnation in Jesus can only be understood together. Both are events of grace, but there is a real difference between them. We remain recipients of God's self-communication. In Jesus grace functions in such a way that this one human being is identified with God's self-offering to the universe.

The incarnation is part of cosmic history. And it is not something arbitrarily decreed by God, an "extra" in evolutionary history. It is not some absolutely new level in the world's reality, unrelated to what was there before. Rather, through God's free choice the incarnation is an inner moment and intrinsic condition for God's bestowal of grace upon the world. It is part of, in fact the climax of, a massive movement of self-transcendence. Viewed from below it is the (asymptotic) goal of the evolutionary history of the world.

Jesus of Nazareth—God's Self-Communication to the Cosmos

So far in this chapter, I have been looking at the event of Jesus of Nazareth from the perspective of the emerging cosmos, and from the perspective of the evolutionary history of the planet.

But, as I have said earlier, in Rahner's theology, the self-transcendence of the cosmos, in its highest stage, is identical with what, from the side of God, can be called God's self-communication. It is necessary to look at the event of Jesus of Nazareth from both sides. It is time, then, to turn from the understanding of Jesus as the outcome of evolutionary history, to reflect upon the incarnation from God's side. In the following few pages I will be exploring the idea that this same Jesus is the definitive self-communication of God to human beings, and through them to the whole cosmos.

Rahner takes the view that creation and incarnation are two

related dimensions of God's self-communication to the world. In saying this, he is consciously choosing one school of theology over another. There are two ancient theological traditions concerning the incarnation in Christian theology, one stressing that the incarnation redeems us from sin, the other stressing that the incarnation was always part of God's plan.

Rahner follows the second approach, which is sometimes called the "Scotist" position after the great medieval Franciscan theologian, Duns Scotus. He situates his evolutionary Christology within this Scotist school of theology which sees the incarnation as the summit of the plan of creation, rather than primarily as the restoration of a world order destroyed by sin.

In his view, then, the incarnation would have occurred even if there had been no sin, and even if there was no need of salvation from sin. It was always God's plan to give God's self to creatures in love through the incarnation. God's self-giving, in Jesus of Nazareth, is primarily to be understood simply as an expression of God's boundless love for creation.

For Rahner, then, there can be no separation between creation and redemption. There can be no theology of creation which is independent of a theology of redemption, and no theology of redeeming grace which is not related to the created world. Creation is "a partial moment in the process in which God becomes world":

> We are entirely justified in understanding creation and incarnation not as two disparate and juxtaposed acts of God "outwards" which have their origins in two separate initiatives from God. Rather in the world as it actually is we can understand creation and incarnation as two moments and two phases of the *one* process of God's self-giving and self-expression, although it is an intrinsically differentiated process.[9]

This is not meant to limit God's freedom and to deny that God could have created a world without an incarnation. Rather it affirms simply that, in fact, God has freely chosen to create a universe in which the Word would become flesh. In this universe, every stage of self-transcendence stands as a free gift of God in relationship to the previous stage, and this is true above all of the incarnation itself.

Rahner insists on the place of sin in this evolutionary view of the world. Although the incarnation would have happened as a free act of love even if there were no sin, in fact we live in a sinful world. The cosmos has evolved in self-transcendence toward spirit and freedom, and "wherever there is freedom in and before the reality of the cosmos as a whole, and in a transcendence towards God, there can also be a guilt and freedom which closes itself against God."[10]

Sin certainly exists in the world. But the world from the start has been based on God's will toward self-communication with creatures in the world. Sin from the outset has been embraced by God's will to offer forgiveness and love to creatures. The redeeming power which overcomes sin is found precisely at the climax of God's self-communication, in the event of the incarnation, above all at its most radical point, the cross and the resurrection of Jesus.

God's explicit communication to human beings occurs within evolutionary history as part of communal and social life. It has a public and historical character. The story of evolution, when it reaches the point of self-consciousness in human persons, is, necessarily, a story of relationships and communication between these persons. The individual subjects in whom the world has come to consciousness are not isolated individuals but communal creatures, sharing a common culture and a common history.

God's self-communication, then, is not something directed simply to isolated individuals, but rather it has a *communal* and *historical* character. Within the common history of the universe, and of humanity, Jesus Christ is to be understood as God's self-communication, expressed in a concrete and irreversible fashion. In this person God's self is given to the world in a tangible, historical form. Through Jesus, and the movement he started, God's self-giving becomes publicly and irreversibly part of human culture, and part of cosmic history.

We human beings experience in ourselves a great hunger for wholeness. Everything good and beautiful in our world opens out toward the whole. Yet our experience of everything is partial. We long for real justice. We search for meaning which satisfies. We yearn for a love which can fill the limitless yearning of our hearts. Our desires are boundless.

This experience of human limits and human brokenness is the experience of a need for the absolute God, a need for salvation. We have within us a taste for the infinite and the whole. We are, as Augustine said, restless beings, who cannot rest except in the One who made us. Rahner's way of saying this is that we are so made as to be recipients of God's self-communication in love. We are finite beings with a limitless openness that can be filled only by being in love with God.

What our very beings need is what Rahner calls the "absolute Savior." The absolute Savior is "that historical person who appears in time and space and signifies the beginning of the absolute self-communication of God which is moving towards its goal, that beginning which indicates that this self-communication for everyone has taken place irrevocably and had been victoriously inaugurated."[11]

This notion of Jesus as absolute Savior should not be understood in such a way as to deny that other religious traditions and figures may be true mediations of God's grace. In fact Rahner has been one of the strongest advocates of the argument that religious traditions other than Christianity may be truly revelatory and truly salvific.[12] But he would maintain that Christians must be faithful to the core of the Christian tradition, just as he would want to respect the core tradition of other great world religions, and part of the core of Christianity is the claim that Jesus of Nazareth is significant for the salvation of all peoples and for the whole world.[13]

There are three dimensions to this notion of the absolute Savior: first, in this person we find God's self-communication given *irrevocably;* second, in this person it is possible *to recognize unambiguously* this self-communication; third, in this person God's self-communication reaches its *climax* in our history. Such an "absolute Savior" would be the irreversible and unambiguous culmination of God's self-giving to the world.

For this to happen two things are necessary: such a person would need to embody not only *God's definitive self-communication,* but also *definitive human acceptance* of this. Only in this way is there truly irreversible self-communication on both sides. Only then would this reality of God's self-giving be in our world in a human, historical and communicable way. This person would be both the absolute promise and self-giving of God, and the human acceptance of this promise and self-gift.

This, of course, is exactly what Christians believe to have occurred in the life, death and resurrection of Jesus of Nazareth. The Jesus who can be known through the gospels, the Jesus who walked through the villages of Galilee preaching and healing, the one who died on the cross and was raised up by God, this Jewish Jesus, child of Mary, is God's irrevocable self-giving to the world. He is unconditional love expressed publicly and unambiguously. He is the climax of God's giving of self in love to the universe.

In this Jesus of Nazareth, we find God giving God's self to the world irreversibly. We also find a part of the world, a human being, the product of evolutionary history, accepting the self-giving God without reservation. Rahner writes:

If the history of matter and spirit in the unity constituted by these two is a history of an ever renewed process of rising to self-transcendence, then the supreme, ultimate, and "eschatological" self-transcendence is that in which the world freely opens itself to the self-bestowal of God himself as Being and Mystery in the absolute, and in which the world accepts this in the power of this self-bestowal of God itself. The acceptance of the world by God in his act of self-bestowal, then, and the acceptance of God in his act of self-bestowal by the world are manifested historically in such a way that these two acceptances are seen to constitute a unity. Moreover this manifestation achieves its irrevocable climax at that point at which these two acceptances become definitive and irrevocable (however much further saving history in general is prolonged). Now if we accept this, then we have precisely accepted what we call the Incarnation of the divine Logos, the Mediator of salvation in the absolute.[14]

The ancient faith of Chalcedon can be expressed anew, then, from within a cosmic and evolutionary context, in the following fashion: In God's self-bestowal in Jesus of Nazareth, first, *God accepts the cosmos definitively and irrevocably,* and, second, *the cosmos accepts God definitively and irrevocably,* and, third, these two acceptances are manifested in our history *as constituting a real unity in the one Jesus of Nazareth.*

This Jesus of Nazareth is a distinct historical individual: the one who was totally centered on a gracious God upholding all creation, the one who interpreted God's law in a "humanizing" way, the one who ate scandalous meals with public sinners, who delighted and challenged his hearers with the artistry of his parables, who taught the impossible, like love of the enemy, the one who vigorously confronted those in authority, the one whose presence brought joy and happiness, the one who called his followers to a new family, the one who faced failure and death because of the positions he took, the one who has been raised up and vindicated by God. This very specific Jesus is the symbol and the reality of God's radical commitment to the cosmos. And this same Jesus is the symbol and the reality of the cosmos returning God's embrace with a definitive "yes."

NOTES

1. John Gribben, *In Search of the Big Bang: Quantum Physics and Cosmology* (London: Corgi Books, 1986) 177.

2. David Ellyard, *Sky Watch* (Crows Nest, N.S.W.: Australian Broadcasting Corporation, 1988) 85.

3. See "Christology Within an Evolutionary View . . . ," 176.

4. See his "Christology in the Setting . . . ," 227.

5. *Foundations of Christian Faith,* 196.

6. *Ibid.* 198.

7. This is what Rahner calls "formal causality," whereby God communicates God's own divine reality to the creature, and makes it a constitutive element in the fulfillment of the creature. The absolute being of God can communicate itself to other beings without God thereby ceasing to be transcendent. See Rahner's "Some Implications of the Scholastic Concept of Uncreated Grace," *Theological Investigations 1,* 319–346; *Foundations of Christian Faith,* 116–137.

8. *Foundations of Christian Faith,* 202.

9. *Ibid.* 197.

10. "Christology Within an Evolutionary View . . . ," 185–186.

11. *Ibid.* 193.

12. See, for example, "Christianity and Non-Christian Religions," *T.I.5,* 115–134; "Anonymous Christians," *T.I.6,* 390–398; "Church, Churches and Religions.," *T.I.10,* 30–49; "Anonymous Christianity and the Missionary Task of the Church," *T.I.12,* 161–178; "Observations on the Problem of the 'Anonymous Christian,' " *T.I.14,* 280–294; "Jesus

Christ and the Non-Christian Religions," *T.I.17*, 39–50. Rahner rejoiced
to see his work bear fruit in the Second Vatican Council's teaching that
salvation is not confined to the limits of the church, but reaches out to all
men and women. See *Lumen Gentium* 16, *Gaudium et Spes* 22, *Ad
Gentes* 7, *Nostra Aetate,* 2. In Rahner's judgment this teaching "marked
a far more decisive phase in the development of the Church's conscious
awareness of its faith than, for example, the doctrine of the collegiality in
the Church, the relationship between Scripture and tradition, the acceptance of the new exegesis etc." ("Observations on the Problem of the
'Anonymous Christian,' " 284).

    13. Rahner, it seems to me, would not be prepared to go as far as
Paul Knitter. See his *No Other Name? A Critical Survey of Christian
Attitudes Toward the World Religions* (London: SCM, 1985), and John
Hick and Paul F. Knitter (editors), *The Myth of Christian Uniqueness:
Towards a Pluralistic Theology of Religions* (Maryknoll: Orbis Books,
1987). The work of Knitter, and other theologians like Raimundo Panik-
kar, is an important challenge to Christian theology. Yet, to my mind, it
still has to reckon with Christianity's understanding of Jesus Christ as
universal Savior. I find myself agreeing with Edward Schillebeeckx who
has commented on Knitter's views in the article "The Religious and the
Human Ecumene," in Marc H. Ellis and Otto Maduro (editors), *The
Future of Liberation Theology: Essays in Honor of Gustavo Gutierrez*
(Maryknoll: Orbis Books, 1989) 177–188. Schillebeeckx seeks to go
beyond both "exclusive" and "inclusive" claims for Christianity vis-à-
vis the other religions, and to go beyond both "absolutism" and "relativ-
ism"; he seeks an answer which recognizes the historical limits of Jesus
of Nazareth, and yet accepts that he is universal redeemer.

    14. "Christology in the Setting . . . ," 226–227.

6

Science on the Future of the Universe

Christian faith is directed toward the future. The death and resurrection of Jesus form the basis of the Christian hope in "a new heaven and a new Earth" (Rev 21:1). But science also has something to say about the future of the universe. In the next few pages I will attempt a very brief summary of the way science sees our future, before looking at the same issue from a more theological perspective.

The "Heat Death" of the Universe

The most universal law of physics is the second law of thermodynamics, which tells us that within any isolated system disorder is always on the increase. Things move toward a flat state of equilibrium. Usable energy is depleted. Things run down and wear out. Physicists describe the quantity of disorder in a system by the word entropy. Experiments show that the total entropy in an isolated system increases, but never decreases.

Rooms get untidy, buildings fall down, vegetation dies and decays, people grow old and die. Entropy is all around us. Of course there are many examples of creative activity as well, sometimes called negentropy: people clean house, buildings are constructed, trees grow, babies are born. But still, the physicists remind us, the second law of thermodynamics is not contradicted, because all these creative and positive actions use energy from somewhere else. The concentration of order in one area is paid for by an increase in disorder somewhere else.

The consequence of the second law of thermodynamics for

the whole universe is obvious enough. If the universe has a limited amount of accessible energy (order), and this is being constantly used up, then the universe will eventually die. This is known as the "heat death" of the universe, and it has been discussed by scientists for over a hundred years.

Modern astronomy can observe the birth and the death of stars. Eventually the fuel which powers the nuclear cycle of a star is used up, and the force of gravity causes it to collapse in upon itself. Some stars will first expand into fiery "red giants," and then shrink and cool; they will end up as black dwarf stars. Bigger stars, those which have a mass twice that of our Sun, will die as spectacular supernovae, blowing themselves up brilliantly. They eventually become small, dense neutron stars. Some of the truly massive dead stars will continue to shrink at an escalating rate, ending up as black holes in space, places where gravity is so extreme that nothing, not even light, can get out.[1]

Our Sun is about four and a half thousand million years old. It is about halfway through its life. Eventually it will run out of hydrogen fuel, and begin to burn helium, and then heavier elements, until all potential nuclear fuel is exhausted. All that will be left will be stable elements like iron. During this process the Sun will swell up and its temperature will greatly increase. Its visible surface will have expanded so far from its center that it will swallow up the inner solar system.

At this stage, Carl Sagan writes, "the Sun, ruddy and bloated," will "envelop and devour the planets Mercury and Venus—and probably the Earth as well."[2] The Sun will become a red giant star. In the process the Earth as we know it will be destroyed, the oceans boiled dry, the atmosphere dissipated in space; solid rock may have melted or vaporized. Soon, all the Sun's fuel will be gone, gravity will take over and our Sun will begin to shrink. Over thousands of millions of years the Sun will degenerate into a white dwarf star. Eventually, it will end up as a small, dense, cold black star.

When we look at the larger system of the whole universe it is not clear what the future will be. One scenario is that of the "open" universe. In this picture the universe will continue to expand, but it will run down and cool down. Galaxies will continue to move apart, but within themselves they will condense into giant black holes, which, as Stephen Hawking has explained, will eventually decay through radiation. All solid matter will disintegrate.

Paul Davies tells us that all the structures we now know, which are so full of splendor and activity, are destined to pass away. What will remain will be only "cold, dark, expanding, near-empty space, populated at an ever decreasing density by a few isolated neutrinos and photons, and very little else." He comments: "It is a scenario that many scientists find profoundly depressing."[3]

But there is another possible outcome, that of the "closed" universe. In this scenario the expanding universe will slow down, and then gravity will take over and it will begin to reverse its motion and contract. Galaxies that are now moving apart will begin to move toward each other. The movement will be slow at first, but will accelerate over millions of years, becoming more and more intense, until the whole universe ends up in a "big crunch" which will echo the "big bang" of the beginning. The entire universe then "shrivels into less than the size of an atom, whereupon spacetime disintegrates."[4] Many physicists believe that this is the end of the physical universe: total annihilation in what is called a "singularity."

Science has not yet reached certainty about whether the universe will keep expanding or begin to contract. There is, at present, a near balance between the forces of expansion and the forces of gravitation. It is, of course, precisely this balance which makes our galaxy, our solar system, and life on Earth possible. One of the crucial questions which science has yet to resolve is the gravity of the universe, which, of course, depends upon its density. Stephen Hawking says that the present evidence suggests "that the universe will probably expand forever, but all we can really be sure of is that even if the universe is going to recollapse, it won't do so for at least another ten thousand million years, since it has already been expanding for at least that long."[5]

There are some scientists who speculate that the universe may be oscillating between cycles of expansion and contraction. They argue that the "big crunch" will stop when the contracting universe reaches a certain density, and it will then "bounce" back into a cycle of expansion. They maintain that there have been a whole series of expansions and contractions. In this hypothesis the big bang in which our world began would have been preceded by the big crunch of another world. Of course we could never get any information from earlier worlds since everything would be destroyed.

Stephen Hawking has attempted to combine General Relativity and quantum theory in a new working model of the universe. He proposes a model in which space-time is limited, but which has no boundaries. There would be no edge of space or time, no singularities, either at the beginning or at the end of the world as we know it. He suggests that we think of the universe as a great globe, like the globe of the Earth. As there is no edge of the Earth at the North Pole, so there is no edge or boundary to the universe either at the big bang or the end. In this model, and in all its complex mathematical underpinning, Hawking is attempting to describe the universe completely, including its beginning and its end, in terms of known laws of science.[6]

At present there is not enough evidence to prove or disprove any of these pictures of the future. There will certainly be more evidence appearing as science continues to work toward a unified theory of the universe. What is clear is that, in every conception of science, the world as we know it is coming to an end.

The "Self-Organizing" Universe

It is important to remember that science itself is undergoing enormous change. For three centuries it has been dominated by the Newtonian paradigm of the machine-like universe and the thermodynamic paradigm of the degenerating universe. We are in the midst of a paradigm shift.[7] What is emerging has been called "the new paradigm of the creative universe."[8] It recognizes the progressive and innovative capacity of nature. It studies the capacities of non-linear systems to organize themselves and to break through to new and more complex structures.

It is not yet clear how this new work will influence our thinking about the "heat death" of the universe. There is no suggestion that it will lead to any denial of the reality of increasing entropy and the view that the universe is running down. But at the very least it raises the possibility of new and unforeseen creativity on the part of the cosmos. Ilya Prigogine and Isabelle Stengers suggest that we simply do not know enough to be sure about what will happen: "In spite of the important progress made by Hawking and others, our knowledge of large-scale transformations in our universe remains inadequate."[9]

The standard thermodynamic paradigm gives us a picture of a universe which begins with an extraordinary amount of order and then degenerates. The new paradigm sees creation as an ongoing process. The universe is capable of self-organization: "Instead of sliding into featurelessness, it rises out of featurelessness, growing rather than dying, developing new structures, processes and potentialities all the time, unfolding like a flower."[10] We have yet to discover what this might mean for the future of the universe.

Arthur Peacocke has suggested that we might imagine entropy as a great stream of disorder. This stream generates within itself very large eddies, and within these eddies there is an increase in order and functional organization. There would be no eddies without the stream. Perhaps, he suggests, the eddies are the very point to the stream of entropy. Peacocke concludes his reflections with these words: "Thus does the apparently decaying, randomising tendency of the universe provide the necessary and essential matrix (*mot juste!*) for the birth of new forms—new life through death and decay of the old."[11]

NOTES

1. This statement needs some qualification, since Stephen Hawking has combined general relativity and quantum mechanics to show the existence of radiation from black holes. See *A Brief History of Time*, 99–113.

2. Carl Sagan, *Cosmos* (New York: Ballantine Books, 1980) 188.

3. Paul Davies, *God and the New Physics*, 204.

4. *Ibid.* 205.

5. Stephen Hawking, *A Brief History of Time*, 46.

6. See *A Brief History of Time*, particularly 115–141. Hawking first presented these ideas at a conference on cosmology in the Vatican in 1981. At the very same conference where Hawking was attempting to do away with the necessity for divine intervention in the big bang, Pope John Paul II argued that it was beyond the capacity of science by itself to account for the beginning of the universe.

7. This paradigm shift is described in Ilya Prigogine and Isabelle Stengers, *Order Out of Chaos*.

8. Paul Davies, *The Cosmic Blueprint*, 2.

9. Ilya Prigogine and Isabelle Stengers, *Order Out of Chaos*, 117.

10. *Ibid.* 200.

11. Arthur Peacocke, *God and the New Biology*, 160.

7

Christian Materialism—
The Future of Creation

For behold, I create new heavens and a new earth;
and the former things shall not be remembered
or come into mind.
But be glad and rejoice forever
in that which I create;
for behold, I create Jerusalem a rejoicing,
and her people a joy (Is 65:17–18).

According to much of science the long-term prospects for the universe are bleak. This creates a serious question for theology. John Macquarrie has said that "if it were shown that the universe is indeed headed for an all-enveloping death, then this might seem to constitute a state of affairs so wasteful and negative that it might be held to falsify Christian faith, and abolish Christian hope."[1]

I believe that, in fact, the scientific picture does not falsify Christian faith or abolish Christian hope. On the one hand, in scientific terms, we are only just at the very beginning of our understanding of principles of self-organization in small non-linear systems here on Earth. It is obvious that a system as complex as the universe might yet hold many surprises in store for us.

On the other hand, in theological terms, it is important to note that the foundation of all Christian theology is the conviction that the God of Jesus Christ can and does bring life out of death. John Polkinghorne has suggested that we can see the predicted death of the universe as the cosmic counterpart to the fact that we human beings will certainly die. Just as we believe in the resurrection of the body we can believe in God's fulfillment for the material universe as well. God's power to save embraces not just humanity, but all of creation.[2]

Can we say more than this about our future, and the future of the material universe? In a lecture he gave toward the end of his life Karl Rahner called for an expansion of the theology of redemption in terms of the redemption of the body and the redemption of the cosmos.[3] What he hoped for was a theology of redemption consistent with his Christology within an evolutionary view of the world.

While this kind of theology of redemption is still somewhat undeveloped, there are some important contributions in Rahner's work, particularly in his writing on the body, on time, and on the "new Earth."

Human Bodiliness

As I have already pointed out, Rahner rejects the kind of separation of body and soul that stems from the influence of Platonic philosophy. At the same time, he accepts that we can distinguish these two elements, but always as dimensions of the one united person. The unity of the human person is of such a kind that the theologian can say that an existential cleavage between body and soul is actually impossible. We cannot encounter a separated body or a separated soul.

Our "inwardness" is the inwardness of the one bodily spirit. Our "outwardness" is the expression of the very same bodily spirit. Rahner builds upon a philosophical insight of Thomas Aquinas. Here the human person is not understood as a combination of a separately existing body and a soul. Rather the human person is seen as a unity of spirit and *materia prima*. It is the spirit that "informs" this prime matter. The body is not something added to the spirit. It is "the concrete existence of the spirit in space and time."[4] The body is the very self-expression of the spirit in space and time.

What, then, happens in death when the body dies? The common answer used to be that the soul survives in heaven, separate from the body, until the general resurrection. Rahner could never accept this idea. He believed that it is of the essence of the soul to be related to matter. Because of this we find Rahner arguing, in his early work on the theology of death, that the human spirit, far from becoming acosmic in death, actually becomes pancosmic.[5] In death, he suggests, a person enters into a deeper, more comprehensive relationship with the whole universe. The relationship which the human spirit always had with matter opens out in death to the wider cosmos. The spirit surrenders its limited bodily structure and becomes open toward the universe, becoming in some way "a co-determining factor of the universe" particularly insofar as the universe is the ground of the personal life of other bodily beings.[6] A person who had become pancosmic through death, and thus achieved a real and ontological relationship with the whole cosmos, could be understood to have a real influence within the world.

Rahner found support for this cosmic theology of death in the doctrine of the resurrection of the body. He argued that the tradition of a radical transformation of the body in the final resurrection was congruent with his understanding of the openness to the cosmos attained in death. The acquisition of bodily form in the resurrection would not do away with the relationship to the cosmos. Rather, the glorified body would become the perfect expression of this relationship with the cosmos.

In his later theology, Rahner came to a different theological position on what happens after death. He no longer saw the necessity for an "intermediate state" between an individual's death and the resurrection of the body.[7] Resurrection life could be understood to begin at the moment of death. This did away with the idea of separated spirits altogether, and there was therefore no need for a pancosmic theology of the separated soul in death.

Even in this new view, however, I believe that it can still be said that the resurrection life of the individual and the community beyond death must be understood as is in some way pancosmic. Death is still to be understood as an entrance into a new and deeper relationship with the whole universe, precisely in the experience of resurrection life.

Bodiliness is essential to the human person. Not only is it essential for us as individuals, it is fundamental to our engagement with each other in community. Through the body each individual enters a sphere which does not belong to himself or herself alone. Bodily existence necessarily involves us with other bodily creatures. There is no inwardness in us that is not open to what comes from without. At the very center of our innermost being we still have something to do with other men and women, and with human history, and also with Jesus Christ. His death two thousand years ago took place in a bodily sphere which is still our reality today.

Our human bodiliness connects us with the whole material environment. If we are necessarily such bodily creatures then our environment cannot be a matter of indifference to us. Rahner writes: "Through bodiliness the whole world belongs to me from the start in everything that happens."[8] We are part of the whole, directly and intimately connected with the rest of matter.

Our bodiliness extends us outward. It connects us in mutual interaction with a wider world. Rahner makes the point that we should not see our bodies as simply ending where our skin ends. We are, in some real ways, open systems. We are far from being self-sufficient. We only have to think, by way of example, how much our bodies depend upon the Sun. What would they be like

without the Sun? At this point it is worth recalling the fact referred to earlier, that we are the product of nucleosynthesis in
stars—we are made of stardust.

Rahner, while admitting that his comment is an exaggera-
tion, can say that there is a sense in which we all live in one and
the same body which is the world.[9] We share a common physical
existence. It is this that constitutes the common space between us.
It is this that makes communication and love possible between
free human beings.

This common ground of bodiliness, Rahner says, is something we can love, put up with, or hate. He suggests that we may
be able to think of our final blessedness or our rejection of this, our
heaven or our hell, as determined for us on the basis of how we
accept or reject this common bodily reality.[10] It is also this common ground that can help us understand our relationship with
those who have gone before us, in what we have traditionally
called the "communion of saints."

Christian faith asserts that our common bodily sphere of
existence is itself involved in a dynamic history which will end in
transfiguration.

Are There Other Intelligent Creatures in the Cosmos?

At the end of *Foundations of Christian Faith*, Rahner considers the possibility that there might be creatures in other parts
of the cosmos, creatures who like us are self-conscious and free,
and who are also borne by God's self-communication in grace,
since grace is the reason for creation.

He finds no theological objections to this idea. In envisioning
this possibility, Rahner writes, "we would move towards the idea
that the material cosmos as a whole, whose meaning and goal is
the fulfillment of freedom, will one day be subsumed into the
fullness of God's self-communication to the material and spiritual

cosmos, and that this will happen through many histories of free-dom which do not only take place on our earth."[11]

In one of his later articles, Rahner returned to this idea. He considered that the possibility that life and conscious beings may exist on other planets can no longer be excluded. It would make sense for Christians to think that God, by grace, was inviting these creatures to a supernatural destiny. Evolutionary history would be for them, too, something which culminates in immediacy with God.

What of the incarnation? Can we think of an incarnation of the Word on another planet? Rahner answers that "it cannot be proved that a multiple incarnation in different histories of salva-tion is absolutely unthinkable."[12] Theologians can say nothing more about these hypothetical questions. Rahner simply makes the point that there is no theological reason to rule out the idea of self-conscious beings on other planets.

What about other "angelic" creatures in the cosmos? Are there conscious free minds which influence cosmic events? Many cultures have believed in such beings. Christianity has its tradi-tion of "angels." Karl Rahner argues, however, that it is by no means obvious that a Christian today is bound to believe in angels, either by the Bible or by the history of doctrine.[13]

But, Rahner argues, if such creatures do exist, they are cer-tainly not "pure" spirits with no connection with the material world. He rejects the common neoplatonic idea of angels. If angels exist they are part of the cosmos, with an essential and intrinsic relationship to matter. Rahner suggests that if we think of the human person as one way in which space-time reality comes to self-expression, then we can speculate about angels as being "greater and more differentiated unities of space-time reality than that of the human body and its synthesis and interiorization of materiality."[14]

If angels exist, then, they have a cosmic function. In the vastness of the universe it is not impossible to conceive of evolutionary history as encompassing the emergence not only of human consciousness, not only of conscious beings on other planets, but also of angelic beings with an essential connection to the world of matter. Rahner understands that these beings would be connected with matter in a limited and regional way, but in a way that is different to human bodiliness. They could be understood as principles of unity and order in a material region, which is larger and more differentiated than the human body.[15]

This idea, that there may be cosmic minds with a real relationship with specific regions of matter, is not unrelated to certain speculations of scientists like Paul Davies that a "natural" mind may be at work in the universe as a supreme holistic principle.[16]

A central idea in the quantum theory concerns the unique role of the mind in determining reality. According to the uncertainty principle of Heisenberg, we cannot know where an atom or electron is and how it is moving at one and the same time. Position and motion are mutually incompatible aspects in our knowledge of these particles. What the observer sees depends upon what he or she looks for. According to the great Danish physicist Neils Bohr the atom only sharpens into focus when an observation is made. It materializes when the observer looks for it. The very act of observation determines the behavior of atoms.[17]

The insights of quantum mechanics raise fundamental questions about the relationship between mind and material reality, which are extremely important for theology, but cannot be pursued here. It must be recognized, however, that any connection between Rahner's thoughts on angels and quantum physics is highly speculative! What is certain, and important to the concerns of this book, is that Karl Rahner insists that if angels exist they are part of evolutionary history, and they are intrinsically related to matter. The traditional treatment of angels was surely one of the most thoroughly non-material areas in the history of theology, and Rahner's recent rethinking of it in cosmic terms is an interesting indication of his commitment to a Christian materialism.

Time

Several times Karl Rahner has dealt explicitly with the issue of time and eternal life.[18] He argues against the popular idea of eternal life as time running on endlessly. If eternity is simply a continual succession of one thing after another, then there is nothing definitive, no arriving, simply endless journeying which he would see as a kind of damnation.

Eternal life is more than this. Rahner argues that we can obtain some glimpses of the nature of eternal life through experiences we have within time. If we consider the experience of the life of a flower, or a person, or a community, we find a succession of individual phenomena, but beyond these individual phenomena there is something permanent which persists, making a unified history. This identity which lies behind the changing moments of time is not simply identical with time itself. There is in time something which persists and gives unity and meaning to time.

Again, when we reflect upon the way human beings think about what they experience, we see that they unify and shape time into a history. A human mind gathers past, present and future together into a unified whole, constructing a history. Rahner says that insofar as there is this kind of thought about time, "something happens which does in fact occur in time's course, but as an event which has a peculiar superiority over time, an event intimating eternity."[19]

A third experience, which can give us some insight into eternity, is that of a free decision which involves one's whole person in an irreversible way. When we make a decision which involves complete and final commitment, "time creates eternity and eternity is experienced in time."[20]

These three experiences provide hints of something in time, that yet escapes time. But Rahner holds that it is impossible to imagine, in the concrete, what eternal life will be like. Transformed bodiliness, the new Earth, our community with all the redeemed, all of these escape our imaginative capacities. They remain unknown, filled with the incomprehensibility of God, and God's love.

In fact, theology tells us that our eternity will not only be filled by God, but it will be the definitiveness of what we really make of ourselves by our free choice on this life. It will be the finality of our present life of freedom. If this is so, then this reveals the mysterious depth and richness of our everyday existence. Acts of selfless love, acts of obedience to conscience, acts of fidelity to truth, are of infinite value. Eternity is part of their inner nature. Wherever life is truly lived in faith, hope and love, eternity already truly occurs.

So eternal life is not simply things continuing on after death. It is not a matter of changing horses and then riding on, as if the openness and lack of determination of this life continued. Time is subsumed into its final and definitive reality which is eternity:

> In reality eternity comes to be in time as time's own mature fruit, an eternity which does not really continue on beyond experienced time. Rather eternity subsumes time by being liberated from the time which came to be temporarily so that freedom and something of final and definitive validity can be achieved.[21]

For Rahner, eternity is not an infinitely long mode of time, but it is the mode of the spiritual freedom which has been exercised in time, and has become definitive in death.

Although Rahner does not make it very explicit, it is clear

that space and time are closely linked in this view of eternity. In terms of a post-Einstein physics we cannot arbitrarily separate time and space. We cannot think of God's future, the new Earth, as simply being in place as we know it, without it also being in time. The only logical theological position is to understand future life as a fulfillment of both space (in the new Earth) and time (in eternity) together. The fulfillment of time is also the fulfillment of space.

Rahner does not accept the idea of a physical world continuing on after the end of human collective history. The future of the material universe is intimately linked to the fulfillment of the community of human beings in whom the world has come to consciousness. We are moving toward a fulfillment of the human race which will end history.

The goal of creation is God's self-communication in grace. The whole material cosmos will be subsumed into the fullness of God's self-communication in eternal life, in and through the many histories of free conscious beings here on Earth, and, perhaps, in other parts of the universe.[22]

The New Earth

There is no doubt about the biblical promise of a "new heaven and a new Earth."[23] What this means, Rahner says, is that the world is directed to a point which is not the end of its existence, but the end of its unfinished and continually developing history.[24]

He asks the question: Who can say how far this end is the very "running-itself-to-death" of the universe? Or is a halt called by God's creative Word? This, then, raises the further question: To what extent can these two be understood as ultimately the same thing?[25]

What revelation makes clear is that the history of the world will come to an end, and this will not be a simple ending or annihilation, but the participation of the whole universe in the consummation and divinization of conscious beings.

The material world is not something that becomes superfluous to spiritual beings in their eternal life in God. The human spirit is always a material, incarnate, inner-worldly spirit. It is always a spirit of the cosmos. It is always the cosmos come to consciousness. The resurrection of the body involves the consummation of cosmic history.

The end of the world is a participation of the world in the resurrection of Jesus Christ. His Second Coming takes place at the moment of the perfection of the universe, as it comes to share the reality which Jesus already possesses. Then the risen Jesus Christ will be revealed as the innermost secret of the world and its history, the victory hidden at the heart of cosmic history.

Christianity rejects any vision of the future which does not include the world of matter. The material world cannot be understood to be like a stage on which the drama of human relationship with the divine is played, so that when the play is over the players leave the stage dead and empty and abandoned.[26] Nor can matter be thought of as simply a "launching pad" which will become unnecessary in a further spiritual state of existence. On the contrary, the material world will still be the expression of human spirit, and will participate in the final glorified state of this spirit.[27]

We cannot imagine the how of this bodily and cosmic transformation. Rahner notes that modern physics presents us with many concepts which are beyond imagination, and suggests that this may help us cope with theological ideas which escape imagination. Even though we cannot imagine it, we know that the cosmos will share in the consummation of the kingdom of God. In some ways this has already begun, because God is already at work as a dynamic power at the heart of creation. Rahner can say:

It is no mere pious lyricism when Dante regards even the sun and the other planets as being moved by that love which is God himself as he who bestows himself. The innermost principle of this self-movement of the sun and the other planets towards their consummation, which lies concealed in the incomprehensibility of God as the absolute future, is God himself.[28]

Rahner would be pleased to be called a Christian materialist. He uses confronting language in his attempt to make it clear that the material world really does have a future. He writes that we Christians are "more crassly materialistic than those who call themselves so." In his view we are the "most sublime of materialists" because "we cannot think of any ultimate fulfillment of the human spirit without thinking at the same time of matter enduring and reaching its perfection."[29]

Because matter itself is to be taken up into the final consummation of all things in God, Rahner is not prepared to agree with those scientists who would have the whole material world simply disappear into nothingness through a gravitational collapse. Of course, science can rightly consider various possible ways in which the "heat death" of the universe might occur. But science cannot rule on a transformed resurrection life for the dead, nor on the future of the material universe transformed from within by the power of God.

Christian optimism about the future of matter does not exclude negativity, violence, suffering or increased entropy. All these are already part of our evolutionary history, and they will be part of the future evolution of the universe. In this evolutionary history, we must be prepared to allow for "surprises, defective developments, dead ends," and even for "a total halt to progress as such."[30]

But these will not be the last word, any more than the apparent failure of Jesus, and his death on the cross, were the end of him and his mission. Christian faith, in the face of all pessimism about the future of matter, affirms that, through God's grace, our evolving world can and will arrive at immediacy with God. It affirms that even now it has begun an irreversible stage of its history.

Jesus Christ is God's irrevocable promise of salvation within the evolving cosmos. In the light of Jesus, and God's promise given in him, Christian theology knows that final catastrophe, and a total halt to progress, are not the future of the unfolding universe. The final goal of evolutionary history for free bodily human beings is intimacy with God, a future shared in some way by the whole created cosmos.

What relationship is there between the world which we help to build by our participation and the new Earth? How is the new Earth related to our work, to culture and to science? How is it related to our efforts to create a just and peaceful world? Is all of this simply the place where we prove ourselves? Or is the new Earth directly related to what we are constructing here and now?

Rahner answers that the coming kingdom of God will be the deed of God. This is the standard Christian tradition concerning the end time. The final consummation will not be simply an outcome of what has been planned and worked at by men and women. We face a future which is radically mysterious and uncontrollable, because it is of God.[31]

But Rahner claims, this deed of God can be thought of as the self-transcendence of our own history. Human history, like the history of nature, is to be transformed from within by the power of God. Human history is destined to endure, but it will endure in a radically transfigured form. God's action is free and beyond our calculations or control, but it comes from within.

History itself passes into definitive consummation in God. According to Rahner, "history itself constructs its own final and definitive state." It is not just human beings who endure into eternity, nor is it simply some moral distillation of what they achieve. Rather "that which endures is the *work* of love as expressed in the concrete in human history."[32] Human work and human love have eternal significance. What we do in our history has final and definitive value.

The human vocation, then, is to be true co-workers with God and stewards of creation. The human task of completing creation derives its meaning from the redemptive and divinizing will of God. This applies even to those who do not know the significance of their contributions. Those whose actions are directed toward the good of the cosmos, believers and unbelievers alike, fall under the impulse of grace. Their actions have eternal value.

NOTES

1. John Macquarrie, *Principles of Christian Theology* (London: SCM Press, 1977) 356.

2. John Polkinghorne, *Science and Creation: The Search for Understanding*, 65.

3. See the article "The Christian Understanding of the Redemption," *T.I.21*, 252–253.

4. "The Body in the Order of Salvation," *T.I.17*, 84.

5. Karl Rahner, *On the Theology of Death* (New York: Herder and Herder, 1962) 19. See also his article "The Resurrection of the Body," *T.I.2*, 211.

6. *Ibid.* 22–23.

7. See the article "The Intermediate State," *T.I.17*, 114–124, particularly 119.

8. "The Body in the Order of Salvation," 87.

9. *Ibid.* 88.

10. *Ibid.*

11. *Foundations of Christian Faith*, 445–446. See also "Natural Science and Reasonable Faith," *T.I.21*, 51–52.

12. "Natural Science and Reasonable Faith," *T.I.21*, 51.

13. "On Angels," *T.I.19*, 235–274.

14 *Ibid.* 255.

15 *Ibid.* 264.

16 Paul Davies, *God and the New Physics*, 218–229.

17. *Ibid.* 100–118.

18. See "Theological Observations on the Concept of Time," *T.I.11*, 288–308; "Eternity from Time," *T.I.19*, 169–177.

19. "Eternity from Time," *T.I.19*, 174.

20. *Ibid.* 175.

21. *Foundations of Christian Faith*, 437.

22. *Ibid.* 446

23. "According to his promise we wait for a new heavens and a new earth in which righteousness dwells" (2 Pet 3·13). See Is 65:17; 66:22; Rev 21.1–5. See also the theme of the "new creation" (Gal 6:15; 1 Cor 7:31; 15:45–49, Rom 5:15–19; 8:18–23; Col 3·9; Eph 2:15; 4:22)

24. See the article "The Resurrection of the Body," *T.I.2*, 211.

25. *Ibid.* 212.

26. "Christianity and the 'New Man,' " *T.I.5*, 147.

27. *Ibid.* 148.

28. "Immanent and Transcendent Consummation of the World," *T.I.11*, 289

29. "The Festival of the Future of the World," *T.I.7*, 183.

30. "Natural Science and Reasonable Faith," *T.I.21*, 55.

31 See the article "A Fragmentary Aspect of a Theological Evaluation of the Concept of the Future," *T.I.10*, 235–241.

32 "The Theological Problems Entailed in the Idea of the 'New Earth,' " *T.I.10*, 270.

8

The Risen Christ and the Cosmos— Taking Rahner a Little Further

> For he has made known to us in all wisdom and insight the mystery of his will, according to his purpose which he set forth in Christ as a plan for the fullness of time, to unite all things in him, things in heaven and things on earth (Eph 1:9-10).

Rahner insists that the death and resurrection of Jesus are so closely connected that they constitute one single event. They are two phases of the one reality, so that one cannot be understood without the other. And the death and resurrection of Jesus must be seen as the culmination of his life.

What is the cosmic significance of this event of death and resurrection? What is the relationship between the risen Christ and the evolving cosmos?

It seems to me that at this critical point Rahner's theology is not as developed as it might be. Before Rahner published his evolutionary Christology, Teilhard de Chardin had already developed his synthesis focused on the risen Christ as the Omega point of cosmic history. Teilhard's work was built upon a complex mixture of scientific argument, extrapolation from the evidence of our evolutionary past to build a picture of a converging future, and Christian revelation. Rahner mentions Teilhard's work a number of times, and acknowledges some similarities, but notes that, unlike Teilhard, he writes only as a theologian, using only the common ground available to all theologians.[1]

Earlier chapters of this book have shown how Karl Rahner works out an evolutionary theology which embraces the human

person, God and Jesus Christ. In his major systematic works, however, Rahner does not explore the relationship between the risen
Christ and the cosmos. There is no systematic equivalent to Teilhard's concept of Christ as the Omega point. There is no real
treatment of the Cosmic Christ.

There are some references to this issue in Rahner's writing on
the resurrection, and I will deal with these in the second section of
this chapter. There are also some insightful and poetic observations about the relationship between the risen Christ and the universe, which appear in unexpected places in Rahner's work. It is to
two of these that we turn now.

Insights from Rahner on the Cosmic Christ

In his book *On the Theology of Death* Rahner reflects on the
connection between the death and resurrection of Jesus and the
material universe. He writes: "When the vessel of his body was
shattered in death, Christ was poured out over the cosmos: he
became actually, in his very humanity, what he had always been
in his dignity, the very center of creation."[2] This strikes me as a
rich and important theme that needs to be developed. How is the
risen Christ, "in his very humanity," the center of creation?

In this same book Rahner writes of Jesus that in his death,
understood as a culmination of his whole life, he becomes open to
the whole of cosmic reality. Jesus Christ becomes a permanent
ontological determination of the whole of cosmic reality. The risen
Christ influences and shapes the very being of the material universe. Rahner comments that this might be a way to understand
the meaning of the descent into hell, the lower world of Sheol. The
salvific reality of Christ, which is consummated in death, is built
into the unity of the universe, so that the world is a radically
different place from what it would have been if Christ had
not died.[3]

This human being, Jesus of Nazareth, who is truly of the Earth, truly part of the biological evolution of the universe, has become, in his humanity, the very center of creation. Jesus Christ in his life and death, in his grace-filled human reality, has become a power shaping the whole cosmos.

Another place in which Rahner expresses some of his convictions about the relationship between the risen Christ and cosmic reality is in one of his meditative writings on Holy Saturday. Here the risen Christ is described as the victory hidden in all cosmic reality, at the heart and center of the Earth which Rahner calls "our mother":

> Christ is already at the heart and centre of all the poor things of this earth, which we cannot do without because the earth is our mother. He is present in the blind hope of all creatures who, without knowing it, are striving to participate in the glorification of his body. He is present in the history of the earth, whose blind course he steers with unearthly accuracy through all victories and all defeats onwards to the day predestined for it, to the day on which his glory will break out of its own depths to transform all things He is present in all tears and every death as the hidden joy and the life which conquers by seeming to die. . . . He is there as the innermost essence of all things, and the most secret law of a movement which still triumphs and imposes its authority even when every kind of order seems to be breaking up. He is there as the light of day and the air are with us, which we do not notice; as the secret law of a movement that we do not comprehend because that part of the movement which we ourselves experience is too brief for us to infer from it the pattern of the movement as a whole. But he is there, the heart of this earthly movement and the secret seal of its eternal validity. He is risen.[4]

In these two extracts Rahner expresses two fundamental theological insights: First, through his death and resurrection Jesus

Christ, in his grace-filled *human* reality, has become a power shaping the cosmos; second, the risen Christ is the victory hidden in all cosmic reality drawing it toward its consummation. It is these two insights that I will attempt to take a little further.

The Cosmic Role of the Humanity of Jesus

In his writings on the resurrection, Rahner has several times suggested a line of thought on the enduring role of the humanity of Christ.[5] He recalls the medieval theological view that the glorified humanity of Jesus is the "physical instrumental cause" of our union with God.[6] Both in this life through grace, and in eternal life through glory, our relationship with God occurs only through the humanity of Jesus.

Rahner notes that this opinion has been the occasion of some controversy. Nevertheless, he believes that a contemporary theology needs to retain and develop the idea that the humanity of Jesus has an enduring role in our relationship with God.

In 1953, Rahner had written an article on "The Eternal Significance of the Humanity of Jesus for Our Relationship with God."[7] He began this article by asking the broad question: In our relationship with God, are we simply taken up into the blazing abyss of God, so that all creatures, including Mary, mother of Jesus, and the saints, and even the humanity of Jesus, become inconsequential?

Rahner's answer is to completely reject the idea that in seeking the absolute reality of God we can despise or reject the limited, finite reality of creatures. We are not called to relate to a God without a world. The only God we know is God-with-a-world. Our God is a God of unconditioned love of created reality. To love this God we must also love what this God loves. We are called to love this created world as God loves it. This world of creatures is "divinely and religiously significant before God."[8]

This is the context in which Rahner considers the more particular issue of the humanity of Christ. Here God's relationship with creation reaches its climax. Rahner argues that the humanity of Jesus is always and everywhere our way to God. He writes of Jesus: "This created human nature is the indispensable and permanent gateway through which everything created must pass if it is to find the perfection of its eternal validity before God."[9] Jesus is "the gate and the door, the Alpha and the Omega."

Our union with God occurs not through some purely mystical flights into the absolute, but through Jesus of Nazareth. We meet God in and through "this finite concrete being, this contingent being, who remains in all eternity."[10] The human reality of Jesus, continuing to exist forever as the reality of the Word of God, has eternal significance for salvation. Jesus is now and forever the permanent openness of finite created being to the living God.

God's grace is forever mediated to men and women through the human reality of Jesus Christ. He is the permanent mediator of salvation. All our religious acts go through the humanity of Christ to God. Human experience of God's grace is always experience of the risen Christ. Both our acts of worship toward God, and God's self-giving to us, are mediated by the Word made flesh.

In Rahner's writing on the resurrection, there is a suggestion that this concept might be applied not just to human salvation, but to the cosmos itself. He writes that the resurrection is "the beginning of the transformation of the world," and "in this beginning the destiny of the world is already in principle decided and has already begun."[11]

He holds that there is an intrinsic and ontological connection between the resurrection of Jesus and the renewal of the world, so that Jesus can be understood as the "pledge and beginning of the perfect fulfillment of the world," and as the "representative of the new cosmos."[12] The world is such a unity, physically, spiritually and morally, that the death and resurrection of Jesus, who is a biological part of this material world, must be understood as "the irreversible and embryonically final beginning of the glorification and divinization of the whole reality."[13]

The risen Christ, freed from the limits of bodily existence in this life, is present to the whole world in a new bodily relationship in and through the resurrection. Jesus, in his bodily humanity, is a permanent part of this one world and its evolutionary dynamism. His resurrection is the beginning of the transfiguration of the world.[14]

There are three important principles at work in Rahner's theology which can be brought together at this point: first, the understanding that our relationship with God is permanently mediated through the humanity of Christ; second, the conviction that God's relationship with human beings is always also a relationship with the whole cosmos in and through human beings, who are the cosmos come to self-awareness; third, the concept that the whole cosmos forms a unity with the risen Jesus, so that his resurrection is the beginning of the divinization of the world.

When these three principles are brought together in this way they provide the basis for a further theological assertion: the humanity of Jesus is eternally significant, not just for God's relationship with human beings, but for God's action at the heart of cosmic and evolutionary history.

Not only is it true that the humanity of Jesus is eternally significant for our salvation, this same humanity of Jesus is eternally significant for the whole created universe. Jesus, like us a child of the cosmos, is God's instrument in the transformation of the whole cosmos.

The historically limited and particular Jesus, described in chapter four above, now risen from the dead, has become the means of transfiguration of the universe. The final consummation of matter will take place in and through the concrete and specific humanity of the glorified and risen Jesus. Already our evolving and self-organizing universe is empowered from within by resurrection life, in and through the humanity of the risen Christ.

The Risen Christ as the Dynamism
at the Heart of the Cosmos

It is one thing to affirm that cosmic and evolutionary history are linked to the humanity of the risen Christ; it is another to attempt to show more clearly *how* the risen Christ is connected to the expanding universe and the whole world of matter. There is a further systematic link that needs to be made between the risen Christ and evolutionary history.

Rahner does not make this connection explicitly, although it is implicit in his system. It can be made through linking together our understanding of the risen Christ with the theology, which Rahner has already devel..ped, of God as the power of self-transcendence at the heart of the cosmos.

The link can be made simply enough. It depends upon the unity in Christ of divine and human natures. The classic Christian doctrine of the two natures in the one person means, of course, that we must understand the risen Jesus Christ as consubstantial with the dynamic, absolute being of God.

But, as Rahner has demonstrated, this dynamic and absolute being of God is the power of self-transcendence at the heart of the universe. It is this very divine nature which empowers the evolutionary movement from within. The divine nature of Jesus Christ is precisely the same divine nature which is creatively at work in all cosmic history. It is the power of self-transcendence at the heart of the universe. The risen Christ is radically and permanently one with the absolute being which empowers the universe. Jesus the Jew, born of Mary, like us forged from stardust, is truly the Cosmic Christ.

The mainstream Christian tradition has always taught that creation is the work of the whole Trinity. Thomas Aquinas tells us that . . . Creation must be understood as the work of the divine essence, common to all three divine persons.[15] This is consistent with the theological and doctrinal principle, concerning God's efficient causality with regard to the world, which states that the three persons of the Trinity form one principle of divine action *ad extra*. The whole Trinity then, must be understood as involved in the work of creation.[16]

This does not deny that the inner structures of the divine act of creation is trinitarian. Aquinas goes on to point out how each of the Trinity relates to creation distinctively, in accordance with the trinitarian processions. He explains this by way of an example taken from the workplace. As a person engaged in a craft works from an idea in the mind, and from love in the will, so God creates through the Word and through Love. God the Father creates through the Word and in the Spirit. The press of the divine from within creation is trinitarian.

In his evolutionary theology Karl Rahner has transformed the theological understanding of God's creative action. He has shown how it can be understood as the impulse of the divine from within the evolving universe. This divine impulse, this press of God at the heart of the universe, must be understood, then, as the work of the divine essence of God. It is the work of the whole Trinity. It is therefore the work of the Word.

The second Person of the Trinity, the Wisdom of God, the Word of God, the One in whom all things were created, the One in whom all will be redeemed and made new, is at the heart of the evolutionary movement of the planet, and the process at the unfolding universe. The dynamism from within creation occurs through the Word.

Jesus Christ, the Word made flesh, is not simply the self-transcendence of the universe into God, and God's self-communication to the world. He is not simply the one in whom all things were created. Nor is this Jesus simply the pledge of God's future for all creation. He is not simply the one who is to come. We can go further and make the assertion: Jesus of Nazareth, risen from the dead, is one with the dynamic power at the heart of cosmic processes. The press of the divine from within creation, which springs from the One who is unbegotten generativity, and occurs in the life-giving Spirit, takes place now and always in and through the risen Christ the Liberator and Saviour of the material universe.

We are told at the beginning of John's gospel that the Word was with God at the beginning, and through this Word all things were created (Jn 1:2–3). The press of the divine being from within creation was always directed toward the Word made flesh. In the event of incarnation, this dynamic creative power of divine being is radically united with a specific human being, and through this human being with all of creation.

In the resurrection, Jesus of Nazareth becomes the Cosmic Christ. The risen Christ is the power of the divine at the heart of the creation, but this divine power is now mediated through the humanity of Jesus, the first fruits of the new creation. A sentence of Rahner's which I have already mentioned perfectly captures these ideas: "When the vessel of his body was shattered in death, Christ was poured out over all the cosmos; he became actually, in his very humanity, what he had always been in his dignity, the innermost centre of creation."[17]

This theology of the Cosmic Christ attempts to capture the decisive meaning of Jesus for a new time and a new cosmology. It strives to remain faithful to the insights of the New Testament hymns, which did the same thing for a different time and a different cosmology. They expressed with great power the conviction of the early church that all things were created in Jesus of Nazareth, and that all creation was to be caught up in the resurrection:

> He is the image of the invisible God,
> the first-born of all creation;
> for in him all things were created,
> in heaven and on earth,
> visible and invisible,
> whether thrones or dominions or principalities or authorities—
> all things were created through him and for him.

He is before all things,
and in him all things hold together.
He is the head of the body, the church;
he is the beginning,
the first-born from the dead,
that in everything he might be pre-eminent.
For in him all the fullness of God was pleased to dwell,
and through him to reconcile to himself all things,
whether on earth or in heaven,
making peace by the blood of the cross.[18]

NOTES

1. See "Christology Within an Evolutionary View . . . ," 159–160, 167; "Christology in the Setting . . . ," 218; *Foundations of Christian Faith*, 180.

2. *On the Theology of Death*, 66.

3. *Ibid.* 65.

4. "Hidden Victory," *T.I.7*, 157–158.

5. See Rahner's article "Resurrection: D. Theology," in *Sacramentum Mundi: An Encyclopedia of Theology* 5 (New York: Herder and Herder, 1970) 332–333; "Dogmatic Questions on Easter," *T.I.4*, 124–126, 132–133.

6. See Thomas Aquinas, *Summa Theologiae*, 3.56.1 ad 3.

7. "The Eternal Significance of the Humanity of Christ for Our Relationship with God," *T.I.3*, 35–46.

8. *Ibid.* 41.

9. *Ibid.* 43.

10. *Ibid.* 44.

11. Karl Rahner, "Resurrection: D. Theology," 333.

12. *Ibid.*

13. "Dogmatic Questions on Easter," 129.

14. "Resurrection: D. Theology," 333.

15. Thomas Aquinas, *Summa Theologiae*, 1.45.6.

16. On these issues see Leo Scheffczyk, *Creation and Providence* (New York: Herder and Herder, 1970) 145–153; Michael Schmaus, *God and Creation* (London: Sheed and Ward, 1969) 84–97.

17. *On the Theology of Death*, 66. Some of the ideas developed in this section can be found expressed in the work of Gustave Martelet, who has been much influenced by Teilhard de Chardin. Martelet has developed the relationship between a cosmic Christology and eucharistic theology. See his *The Risen Christ and the Eucharistic World* (London: Collins, 1976), particularly 160–179. In quite a different way Peter Chirico also treats the relationship between the risen Christ and the cosmos as part of his theological system. See his *Infallibility: The Crossroads of Doctrine* (Wilmington: Michael Glazier, 1983), particularly 66–85 and 125–136.

18. Col 1:15–20; see also 1 Cor 8:6; Phil 2:5–11; Eph 1:3–14; Heb 1:1–3; Jn 1:1–18; 1 Jn 1:1–4.

9

Conclusion

This book has been an attempt at working toward a theological response to both the ecological crisis we face and the new cosmology we are learning.

I have been proposing that the tradition of Karl Rahner has much to offer in this context. There are some key insights in his work that can help us come to a fresh and creative response to the story of the cosmos, in the light of the story of Jesus of Nazareth.

Perhaps it might be helpful to gather some of these insights together at the end of this work before making some comments on the relevance of this cosmic theology for the end of the second millennium.

A Synopsis

1. *The whole cosmos has a fundamental unity in the one God, who creates it, sustains and empowers it, and brings the whole to completion.* Matter, life, and consciousness form one single history of evolution. Each development, however, is new and essentially different from the preceding stage.

2. *The human person can be understood to be the cosmos itself come to self-consciousness.* It is of the nature of matter to develop toward consciousness, and the material universe achieves its own self-awareness in human persons, and in human community. The history of the universe continues in the human community, in culture, and in human interaction with the Earth. *This evolutionary history of the cosmos reaches its goal in God's self-communication by grace to conscious beings, and through them to the whole cosmos.*

3. *Evolutionary change is empowered and sustained through the dynamic impulse of the divine being operating from within creation.* This is what Rahner calls "active self-transcendence." This notion implies, first, that evolutionary shifts occur through a power that is genuinely intrinsic to the creature, and, second, that this power belongs not to the nature of the creature but to God.

4. *In Jesus of Nazareth, in his life, death and resurrection, the universe reaches the climax of its history of self-transcendence toward God.* In this one person's "yes" to God, evolutionary history reaches its goal, a goal it could never attain of itself. This Jesus is part of the history of the cosmos, truly of the Earth, truly a moment in the biological evolution of the universe. What has been called from the side of matter, the self-transcendence of the cosmos, is identical with what can be described from God's side as God's definitive self-communication.

5. *There is an intrinsic and necessary connection between God's self-communication in Jesus and God's universal self-communication through grace.* The self-transcendence of the world into God takes place not only in Jesus but in all spiritual beings. The effect of the incarnation on the humanity of Jesus occurs through the same grace offered to us. What constitutes the uniqueness of Jesus is that, unlike us, Jesus *is* God's offer. The incarnation must be understood as an inner moment of God's self-giving to the world through grace.

6. *Jesus of Nazareth is God's absolute self-communication to the cosmos.* Creation and redemption are understood as two moments in the one process of God's self-communication with the world. Within the history of the cosmos, Jesus can be understood as the absolute Savior: in him God's self-communication reaches its climax in our history, and is given irreversibly and unambiguously. In Jesus of Nazareth, God accepts the cosmos, and the cosmos accepts God, and these two acceptances constitute a unity.

7. *Bodiliness is essential to human beings, and our eternal life involves transformed bodies and bodiliness.* The body can be

understood as the self-expression of the spirit in space and time. Through our bodies we are necessarily related to others, and to the whole cosmos, in a common sphere. We are open systems, in some sense inhabiting one world body. The glorified resurrection body involves a bodily relationship with the whole cosmos.

8. *Eternal life is time subsumed into its definitive state.* It is not time running on endlessly. It is not an infinitely long time. It is not a matter of "changing horses and riding on." Eternal life comes to be as "time's mature fruit." It is the finality of our own free acts in time. It is the achievement of something definitive and final. It is filled with the incomprehensible mystery of God, and God's love.

9. *The whole of creation, the whole cosmos, will share in the consummation of all things in Christ.* The material universe will itself be transformed. There will be a new Earth. The coming kingdom will be God's deed, but it will also be the self-transcendence of our cosmic history. Our own action and our own loving have eternal significance. The human task of caring for and completing creation has final salvific significance.

10. *Through his death and resurrection Jesus of Nazareth has become an "intrinsic principle" and a "determining feature" of the whole cosmos.* In his death and resurrection Christ has been poured out over the cosmos and "become actually, in his very humanity, what he has always been in his dignity, the very centre of creation." He is the beginning and the pledge of the future of the material universe. The risen Christ is the power and the victory hidden in all cosmic reality, drawing it toward its consummation in the new Earth. He is the divine power of self-transcendence at the heart of cosmic processes.

The Integrity of Creation, the Value of the Person, and Cosmic Praxis

These reflections have made it clear that there is a great deal of insight to be gained by pondering Rahner's theology in the light of the "new cosmology" of the late twentieth century. Cosmic thinking is no mere addendum to Rahner's work. It is intrinsic to the flow of it, more intrinsic than most casual readers would think. Rahner takes matter seriously.

Rahner, of course, also takes Jesus of Nazareth seriously. His theology is capable of connecting our cosmic concerns with a profound Christology. I believe that this answers a great need of our times. There are a number of religious thinkers and writers who seem almost to have abandoned Christianity and its central doctrines concerning Jesus Christ and our salvation, and moved toward a general "world religions" approach to cosmic issues. This approach also has its place, of course. It is easy to understand and share the concerns of those who claim that the Christian west has led the way in the destructive exploitation of the Earth. There is no doubt that the Christian tradition has been used as justification for an irresponsible plundering of our planet.

It seems to me, however, that this makes it all the more urgent that we rethink our theology critically. I am convinced that we can find, within the Jewish and Christian traditions, the foundations for a creative approach to the great cosmic questions posed by science and by the ecological crisis. We Christians need to think again about the universe and our care for the Earth in the light of Jesus of Nazareth. What is needed is a courageous and systematic rethinking. Karl Rahner has already shown the way.

Bringing together the story of Jesus of Nazareth and the story of the cosmos in the way that I have been doing in this book has certain consequences. I will draw attention to three of them.

The first is what is sometimes called the principle of the *integrity of creation*. If we are profoundly related to all of creation, forming one world with all living things, and with the whole material universe, if we are related as "companions" to other creatures, if we are responsible before the God of creation for our interaction with these creatures, if we are called to love the world as God loves the world, if this whole material world is to be taken up into the consummation and share in the resurrection, and if Jesus Christ is at the heart of the whole evolving world, then we are committed to attend to the ecological whole when we act in any one area of the planet.

Thomas Aquinas taught that great variety and diversity of creatures expresses something of the abundance and goodness of God,[1] and some contemporary theologians understand the whole of creation as a kind of sacrament of God.[2] An authentic Christian theology commits us to care for the Earth, and for every creature on it. The evolutionary and cosmic Christology developed in this book grounds a fundamental ethical principle for our time: respect for the whole biosphere, and respect for the integrity of all creation.[3]

The second of these principles concerns *the dignity and value of the human person.* This, of course, is not a new principle. It has long been one of the bases of Christian social ethics. But there are those who are concerned about ecology who tend to devalue human beings, treating them simply as one species among others. The theology developed in this book supports another position. It sees the human person, and the human community, as profoundly inter-related with all other creatures, but in such a way that the human person is understood as the cosmos come to consciousness. Furthermore, the human person is understood as the recipient of God's self-communication. The goal of evolutionary history is the self-giving of God to women and men, and through them to the whole cosmos.

This kind of theology commits us to both respect for the integrity of creation and respect for the unique dignity of the human person. It supports a social ethics which combines care for the Earth with solidarity for the poor of the Earth. It commits us to seeing economic oppression, sexism and racism as intrinsically inter-related with the violation of our planet.

In an evolutionary vision like the one described in this book, developing economic and social conditions which are just, and learning to manage our interactions with the ecosystem of the planet in the cause of life itself, are both understood as related dimensions of the evolutionary role of women and men at this time.

Finally, this kind of theology is a challenge to be engaged with the cosmos. It is an invitation to a *cosmic praxis*. The concept of praxis is a common one in theology these days. It refers to our participation in the shaping of the world in which we live. It is based upon the idea that we are meant to make a difference. We are called to be contributors, people of reflection and action.

The arguments developed here suggest that all our action and reflection needs to take place in a global, and even a cosmic, perspective. We cannot retreat to some earlier ideal relationship with nature. What we can and must do is test all our actions against an intelligent assessment of their impact on the biosphere. We are answerable before God for our care of the Earth. It is our responsibility to undo as much as we can of the damage already done, and to contribute creatively to saving the planet and enriching its future.

This is our common human task. It is our call to be participators in God's continuous creation. Our action and our love at this moment have final significance for God's future, a future which will grow out of the world we make, through the transforming power of God:

> Then I saw a new heaven and a new earth; for the first heaven and the first earth had passed away, and the sea was no more. And I saw the holy city, a new Jerusalem, coming down out of heaven from God, prepared as a bride adorned for her husband; and I heard a great voice from the throne saying, "Behold, the dwelling of God is with people. He will dwell with them, and they shall be his people, and God himself will be with them; he will wipe away every tear from their eyes, and death shall be no more, neither shall there be mourning nor crying nor pain any more, for the former things have passed

away." And he who sat upon the throne said, "Behold, I make
all things new" (Rev 21:1–5).

NOTES

1. "For he brought things into being in order that his goodness
might be communicated to creatures and represented by them. And
because his goodness could not be represented by one creature alone, he
produced many different creatures so that what was wanting in one in
the manifestation of the divine goodness might be supplied by another.
For goodness, which in God is simple and uniform, in creatures is mani-
fold and divided. Hence the whole universe together participates in the
divine goodness more perfectly and represents it better than any single
creature whatever" (Thomas Aquinas, *Summa Theologiae* 1.47.1).

2. See, for example, Michael J. Himes and Kenneth Himes, "The
Sacrament of Creation: Towards an Environmental Theology," *Commonweal* (Jan. 26, 1990) 42–49.

3. In his *Message for the World Day of Peace* (January 1, 1990)
Pope John Paul II said: "We cannot interfere in one area of the ecosystem
without paying due attention both to the consequences of such interfer-
ence in other areas and to the well-being of future generations" (par. 6).
He also said: "No peaceful society can afford to neglect either respect for
life or the fact that there is an integrity to creation" (par. 7). This important message has been published in booklet form under the title *The
Ecological Crisis: A Common Responsibility* (Washington, D.C.: United
States Catholic Conference, 1990).